CARRYING WATER TO THE FIELD

Ted Kooser Contemporary Poetry

EDITOR
Ted Kooser

CARRYING WATER TO THE FIELD

New and Selected Poems

JOYCE SUTPHEN

Introduction by Ted Kooser

University of Nebraska Press | Lincoln

Poems from *Straight Out of View* © 1995, 2001 by
Joyce Sutphen. Poems from *Naming the Stars* ©
2004 by Joyce Sutphen. All used by permission of
The Permission Company, Inc., on behalf of Holy
Cow! Press, www.holycowpress.org. Acknowledg-
ments for the use of other copyrighted material
appear on pages xi–xii, which constitute an exten-
sion of the copyright page.

Publication of this volume was made possible in
part by the generous support of the H. Lee and
Carol Gendler Charitable Fund.

Library of Congress
Cataloging-in-Publication Data
Names: Sutphen, Joyce, author. |
Kooser, Ted, author of introduction.
Title: Carrying water to the field: new and
selected poems / Joyce Sutphen;
introduction by Ted Kooser.
Description: Lincoln: University of
Nebraska Press, [2019] | Series:
Ted Kooser Contemporary Poetry
Identifiers: LCCN 2019005282
ISBN 9781496216366 (pbk.: alk. paper)
ISBN 9781496217332 (epub)
ISBN 9781496217349 (mobi)
ISBN 9781496217356 (pdf)
Classification: LCC PS3569.U857 A6 2019 |
DDC 811/.54—dc23 LC record available at
https://lccn.loc.gov/2019005282

Set in Scala OT by E. Cuddy.
Designed by L. Auten.

For my family, near and far

CONTENTS

ACKNOWLEDGMENTS

Poems selected from *Coming Back to the Body* are reprinted by permission of Joyce Sutphen. Many thanks to Holy Cow! Press for publishing *Coming Back to the Body* (2000). Poems from *Straight Out of View* (2001) and *Naming the Stars* (2004) are reprinted by gracious permission of Holy Cow! Press. Many thanks to Red Dragonfly Press for permission to reprint poems from *First Words* (2010), *After Words* (2013), and *Modern Love & Other Myths* (2015), and thanks also to Salmon Poetry for kind permission to reprint poems from *The Green House* (2017).

I wish to thank the following journals and collections in which the poems selected from *Straight Out of View, Coming Back to the Body, Naming the Stars, First Words, After Words, Modern Love & Other Myths*, and *The Green House* first appeared, a few in slightly different versions: *Agassiz Review, American Poetry Review, Artword Quarterly, Atlanta Review, Bareroot Review, Birmingham Poetry Review, Bloomsbury Review, Blueroad Reader, Caffeine Destiny, Cape Rock, Dickinson Review, Dogwood, Dust and Fire, Flurry, Georgia State Review, Gettysburg Review, Great River Review, Green Blade, Hayden's Ferry Review, Kean Review, Knockout, Lake Region Review, Lascaux Review, Loonfeather, Luna, Magma, Marge, Minnesota Artists Online, Minnesota English Revue, Minnesota Monthly, Minnesota Poetry Calendar, North Coast Review, Northeast Review, North Dakota Review, North Stone Review, Passages Northwest, Peregrine, Poetry, Rag Mag, The Same, Scread, Seminary Ridge Review, Shenandoah, Sidewalks, Slant, Speakeasy, Spoon River Poetry Review, Three Candles, Turtle, Twin Cities Review, View from the Loft, Vincent Brothers Review, Visions International, Water~Stone Review, Whistling Shade, The Wolf*.

Many thanks to the following journals and places where the new poems were first published: *Great River Review, Gustavus Quarterly, Rain Taxi, Rhino, Split Rock Review, What's Left*, and *Undocumented: Great Lakes Poets Laureate on Social Justice* (Michigan State University Press, 2019).

Special thanks to the newspaper column, American Life in Poetry and to the radio programs *The Writer's Almanac, A Prairie Home Companion*, and *Poetry from Studio 47* for presenting poems that appear in this collection. Thanks as well to the Jerome Foundation, the McKnight Foundation, the Loft Literary Center, the Minnesota State Arts Board, and Gustavus Adolphus College for their generous support and gratitude to the Anderson Center in Red Wing, Minnesota, the Djerassi Foundation in California, and the Writer's House in County Clare, Ireland, for residencies where some of these poems came into being.

My deepest gratitude goes to Ted Kooser, Connie Wanek, Phil Dentinger, Tim Nolan, and Walt Cannon—all of whom provided invaluable help with the selections (old and new) and whose astute comments and wise advice always improved the text. I am also grateful to Walt for his generous help in proofreading the manuscript and for his unflagging support. Thanks to more friends than I can name who keep the midwestern poetry community strong, and to Bill Holm, Phebe Hanson, John Rezmerski, and Carol Bly, whose voices I'll never forget.

INTRODUCTION

Ted Kooser

You may have seen a reproduction of a famous self-portrait from 1822, *The Artist in His Museum*, by Charles Willson Peale. It depicts the eighty-one-year-old Peale, in black formal wear, posed at the entrance to his Philadelphia museum of curiosities, standing among things he's collected and wants us to see. With one raised hand he lifts a red curtain in welcome, behind which is a great hall full of natural history displays that recede into the distance.

I've been reminded of Peale's painting while reading and rereading the book in your hands, which too offers a welcome and invites us into a world. In this instance we aren't to stroll past glass-fronted cases of bones and stuffed birds but rather a collection of moments that may feel quite familiar to you, that may not be exotic, but which illuminate the pleasures and pains of lives we and the poet are sharing.

Nebraska's Willa Cather created several female characters who had humble beginnings but through will and industry were lifted into success in the arts. So too Joyce Sutphen, who was raised on a family farm in Stearns County, Minnesota, the oldest of nine children, and who went on to become a college professor, a Shakespearean scholar, a mother and grandmother, and is the current poet laureate of her state, the second to be so named, after Robert Bly.

As she drove past the orchards and fields between her home and her work at Gustavus Adolphus College, Sutphen memorized hundreds of poems, from Donne to Dickinson to Yeats and Symborska, and as she'd tell you, internalizing these rhythms and images shaped how she wrote and even who she is. She was collecting the tools she would need and was learning to use them. And to use them until all their handles were shining.

The poets of Nebraska, Kansas, and the Dakotas live out on the fringed edge of the beautifully woven Minnesota literary community of which Sutphen is an important and essential part, a group which I, for one, have always wished I could be part of. At the center—sixty, seventy years ago—were Robert and Carol Bly, James Wright, Meridel Le Sueur, Fred Manfred. At Manfred's literary gatherings, his "Cornstalks" at his home in Luverne, at the Bly farm in Madison, and at conferences in Marshall and elsewhere, young people were welcomed into the circle, helped and encouraged. I had as a student a fine young poet whose parents took her as a toddler to those gatherings at Manfred's, and the course of her life was forever changed. That original circle grew and spread, but not a single thread was plucked out and discarded. Today what I think of as that community includes all their dead, too, gone but not absent, still part of that lovely, steady friendship. For them Bill Holm is still alive and laughing, loudly, and John Rezmerski is reciting his poem with its terrible Tarzan yell at the center. Phebe Hansen, gone for a couple of years, is still creating an exuberant stir. How much they enjoy each other, the living and dead.

Am I deluded in imagining that the Minnesota writers are friends, really friends, wholeheartedly supporting each other? I think not. Joyce Sutphen's poems open their arms and pull us into that kinship. Her poetry contains the best of them all, their warmth toward one another, their talent for setting down just the right words, their humility under the great universe wheeling above, and the wisdom to live their lives deeply and fully without making too much of a stir. And who but she could write, with complete knowledge of her subject, an ode to the oat binder?

In these pages are poems about family, the land, travels and travails, poems about love and death. Here are sonnets and elegies and meditations upon our frailties and our strengths. Within these pages is everything good about Minnesotans and Minnesota writing, and also about all of us who may live far beyond the edges of that sunny flat place with its clear shallow lakes, the center of something remarkably sound. At this entrance to her compelling museum she lifts the great curtain and we are invited to see what she loves.

CARRYING WATER TO THE FIELD

SELECTIONS FROM *STRAIGHT OUT OF VIEW*

Straight Out of View

I'm thinking of birds—not only white ones.
I'm thinking of all the birds in the *Golden Book of Birds*,
and of their nests, and the parts of the country
where they're likely to be found.

Tepees and moonlight,
I'm thinking of owls and winter roads,
of quiet smoke ascending,
twisting out of the skin cone.
Shadows, rocking against the fire.

Chamomile and honeybees,
netted masks, and keeper's gloves.
Queens and drones and mysterious
dancing under the basswood leaves.
I'm thinking these wooden boxes,
the smooth-jointed edges of the hive,
are grayed like no other coffin.

Three-legged dogs and marshes,
tall reedy places where blackbirds wing.
Flaming eyes in the hillside,
the dragon kiln stoked and breathing fire.
A black kiss smothers the clay.

I'm thinking of ink,
letters fading,
and words that are fragile.
They begin to fly away as birds do:
suddenly, straight out of view.

The Farm

My father's farm is an apple blossomer.
He keeps his hills in dandelion carpet
and weaves a lane of lilacs between the rose
and the jack-in-the-pulpits.
His sleek cows ripple in the pastures.
The dog and purple iris
keep watch at the garden's end.

His farm is rolling thunder,
a lightning bolt on the horizon.
His crops suck rain from the sky
and swallow the smoldering sun.
His fields are oceans of heat,
where waves of gold
beat the burning shore.

A red fox
pauses under the birch trees,
a shadow is in the river's bend.
When the hawk circles the land,
my father's grainfields whirl beneath it.
Owls gather together to sing in his woods,
and the deer run his golden meadow.

My father's farm is an icicle,
a hillside of white powder.
He parts the snowy sea,
and smooths away the valleys.
He cultivates his rows of starlight
and drags the crescent moon
through dark, unfurrowed fields.

Tornado Warning

That is not the country for poetry.
It has no mountains, its flowers
are plain and never poisonous,
its gardens are packed into blue mason jars.
There are no hedges bordering the roads, the sky
flies up from the ditches, loose in every
direction.
    Yet I knew it to be passionate,
even in its low rolling hills, where a red
tractor pushed through the oat field, cutting
down gold straw and beating a stream
of grain into the wagon trailing behind
in the stubble.
    I knew it to be melodious
in its birch woods, leaves shadowing
a stone-strewn river, the path along the bank
softened with pine needles, sunlight
woven in and out of branches, the many
colors of green, solid as a pipe organ's
opening chord,
    I knew it would haunt
the memory with its single elm,
where a herd of cows found shade
in the July heat, their bony tails
swinging the tufted bristle left and right
over the high ledge of a hip bone,
while at the horizon, a black fist
of storm came on, something not
to be averted, something singular
in its fury,
    as any blind heart knows.

Feeding the New Calf

The torso comes out slick and black,
after hoofs that are yellowed
like smoker's teeth, the back
two legs crossed over each other and
the head last, bunched over front legs.

Minutes later he is standing wobbly,
and the blunt mouth is sucking at my arm,
tongue rough as sandpaper, tickling along my
skin, ripping up the fine hair over my wrist.
I tie him with a rope of bailing twine,

Shake out a chunk of straw around him,
as the dust rises in the sunlit aisle. I pet
the wet coat that curls over his sharp
backbone, scratch ears that are thick as
tulip leaves, bent in the womb. Angus baby.

I think of the blue-gray afterbirth, like a shawl
he wore, now left in the gutter, of his mother,
how she groaned him out of her belly, her back
rocking back and forth in the metal stanchion,
the velvet fold of her throat on the cold cement.

After I pour the milk into a pail, I go to
where he is lunging on the rope, where he is
singing a desperate duet with his mother:
din of soulful mooing. I get him to suck
at the nipple, pulling his mouth over to it
with my hands dipped in his mother's milk,
my small solid fingers and not her warm udders,
no peach-veined bag to sink his cheek on.

The clouds sunk in his large brown eyes
float blue. He nudges me, hard.

My Father Comes to the City

Tonight his airplane comes in from the West,
and he rises from his seat, a suit coat slung
over his arm. The flight attendant smiles
and says, "Have a nice visit," and he nods
as if he has done this all before,
as if his entire life hasn't been 170 acres
of corn and oats, as if a plow isn't dragging
behind him through the sand and clay,
as if his head isn't nestling in the warm
flank of a Holstein cow.

Only his hands tell the truth:
fingers thick as ropes, nails flat
and broken in the trough of endless chores.
He steps into the city warily, breathing
metal and exhaust, bewildered by the
stampede of humanity circling around him.
I want to ask him something familiar,
something about tractors and wagons,
but he is taken by the neon night,
crossing carefully against the light.

St. Joe, the Angelus

And so the bells came and summoned us
up and down the street so main it had
no name, calling us from the green benches
in front of Linneman's General Store,
across the cyclone fence of playground
and the pipe-framed doors that rang even
like bells when they closed behind us,
the U-shaped bracket clanking into place
around the silvery pole. And so we walked,
still ringing down the street into Loso's,
painted red in its shady second-best
reputation, its wooden floors bent and
rippling toward the cash register,
and into the cool granite of the bank,
the green billiard light of the Midway,
the butcher's shop, and Jaren's Drugstore,
where a girl lingered at the magazine rack,
leafing out in lipstick dreams, her skin
tanning quietly, her fingernails glistening,
and then past the rolling red-and-white
stripe of the barbershop, where we learned
the word "leukemia" and across to where
the professor lived with his faint disdain
and his wild-haired children, all the way
over the broken edge of sidewalk and through
the arc of lawn sprinklers to my grandmother's
chrome table, the chip of gold-and-blue plate,
potatoes frying in butter, pickles in the dish,
and then exactly at the pause of noon, the Angelus.

In Black

The image that haunts me is not beautiful.
I do not think it will open into a field
of wildflowers; I doubt that it will take
wing suddenly, startling us into admiration.

It is one of those brutish facts of life,
the awkward nakedness of the memory when
it takes off its clothes and crawls
between the top and bottom sheet. Or rather,

it is my mother's memory that I carry,
pressed into my own: how at her grandfather's
funeral, his daughter—my mother's mother—
stood at an open door and cried, and then

The blood ran down her legs, gushing from
the womb where thirteen children had nestled,
and now, at once horrified and at ease with her
body's impropriety, they gathered all around.

This was the grandmother who lost three of those
thirteen, who hung a million baskets of wash,
who peeled a million potatoes, and splattered
her arms with the grease of constant cooking.

This was my grandmother who kept chickens,
who left her voice in the throats of all my aunts,
and was struck down in the cellar, legs twisted
beneath the fall and half her face stiffened.

Helpless until they found her, the jar
of canned fruit smashed on the cement.
And then at her funeral, I saw my mother's
tears, gliding ahead of me in a black limousine,
a procession not beautiful but haunting.

From Out the Cave

When you have been
at war with yourself
for so many years that
you have forgotten why,
when you have been driving
for hours and only
gradually begin to realize
that you have lost the way,
when you have cut
hastily into the fabric,
when you have signed
papers in distraction,
when it has been centuries
since you watched the sun set
or the rain fall, and the clouds,
drifting overhead, pass as flat
as anything on a postcard;
when, in the midst of these
everyday nightmares, you
understand that you could
wake up,
you could turn
and go back
to the last thing you
remember doing
with your whole heart:
that passionate kiss,
the brilliant drop of love
rolling along the tongue of a green leaf,
then you wake,
you stumble from your cave,
blinking in the sun,
naming every shadow
as it slips.

Great Salt Lake

The clouds on the horizon brought
a storm later that night, but here
they are lovely, rubbing their dark
knuckles over the yellow dunes,
flickering slivers of lightning
into the sage-green water.
Plagues of midges sweep the salt-white beach;
coppered snakes swirl in the silken lake.

Still we go in. We make this one
pilgrimage, and though we try to sink,
we stay afloat, supported by ropy
fingers that leave ghost traces
on our skins. We think we hear
a choir singing. Eventually, we grow
tired of skimming the surface
and wash the brine from our bodies.

Night, we roll into sleep
and dream of coyotes, of rattlers,
of door handles breaking off
in our hands, the brittle
chrome of our first fears.

Holland Park at Dusk

Across the gardens—where one shade of green
layered itself against another darker and
still another lifted its frosted almost blue-
green to the palest yellow—there was a peacock on the wall,
his unearthly call breaking the flutter of sweeter wings.
Excellent birds in the overleafing sky.

I don't know how the sun, a brightness
hidden behind the peacock's wall, filled the
chestnut leaves, or how each seven-rayed
cluster shadowed bright in the evening breeze,
but I saw how deeply those pieces of the world
held up the spaces between each other.

I heard a clarinet playing "Darling Where Is Your Heart?"
and three men talked of springtime and parted
one by one. Children played under the trees.
Grandmothers walked. Even when the man from the café
came out with his broom and swept away the day—
even then, I couldn't move away.

Riding East to Dover

From our window we saw the yellow rapeseed fields
covering the plains of Kent and drank
our filtered coffee and ate our Bramley
pies. Kent, sir—everybody knows Kent:
Apples, cherries, hops, and women, said Mr.
Jingle. And still the hopfields, and still
some ancient oast houses, their cone hats
surprising the horizon. My companion, affable
but complaining of filmy windows, stretched
his legs and noticed the oak trees downed by
winter storms, predicted the deforestation of
the few remaining treestands in Britain, was
gleeful despite his visions, cheered by
the prospect of imminent derailment, or at
least a long halt just outside of some paint-
blistered town on the Kentish Downs, where little
back gardens shouldered up to each other, glass
houses sheltering clay pots, rakes, and hoes
glinting dully, the cement crumbling into weeds.

Reading Sylvia Plath in London

You frighten me.
It is hard to read your words
and hear the stories of black London days:
the desperate mix of hope and hate,
the never-quite-right way to live,
and always, aren't we to blame?
Nothing enough or close to perfect
except for, possibly, describing
the coldness of the kill or the peaceful cruelty
of a self-inflicted final scene, which
still unravels and comes back,
enshrouded and laserlike
in a trail of confusion,
wearing out the soul
with its weary chant:

    Deliver us from
    warm milk,
    from chipping paint,
    the gas-blue flame,
    the hiss,
    the hum,
    the sinking eye,
    gray morning fog.

And now the Thames to the south,
the Tower and ravens to the east,
and your words spreading
over the Unreal City,
a deeper shade of grief.

Edgar's Dream

And always I can imagine myself back
into that part of London, as if
coming up the steps of the Underground
and turning into the quick familiar street,
the mail pillar thick with red paint,
birds settling on the window ledges,
even flying into our kitchen to eat crusts,
flapping against the sunlit floor and then
back out to the narrow street, the bluest
skies in three centuries between the rooftops.

Sunday afternoons in the park, watching
the rowers and the peacocks spreading
their plumes when I leaned over the rail.
Walking the path under chestnut trees,
people resting on the benches,
dogs, children, cricket on the green,
shouts floating overhead like kites,
the pleasure of walking under the arch
where teenagers listened to Pink Floyd.

I hoped they would remember me, my notebook
and cappuccino, how I saw for hours watching
the children feed pigeons, indulgent in
this life across the globe, always careful
not to lose myself or stand too close to the edge
of the conjured up cliff, where I could see
fishermen small as mice on the beach below
and the birds wheeling, halfway down.

Death Becomes Me

Death has been checking me out,
making himself at home in my body,
as if he needed to know his way
through the skin, faintly rippling
over the cheekbone to the hollow
beneath my eyes, loosening
the tightly wound ligaments
in the arm, the leg,
infirming the muscle
with his subtle caress,
traveling along the nerve,
leaping from one synapse
to the next, weaving his dark threads
into the chord that holds me tall.
Death is counting my hair,
figuring out the linear equation
of my veins and arteries,
the raised power
of a million capillaries,
acquainting himself with the
calculus of my heart,
accessing the archives
of memory, reading them
forward and backward,
finding his name everywhere.
Death comes to rest in my womb,
slaking away the rich velvet
of those walls, silently halting
the descending pearls,
as if he could burrow in
and make himself my mother,
as if he could bare my bones
and bring me to that other birth.

Suppose Death Comes Like This

Suppose it is the sound of a window opening,
the scrape of wood against wood and the
weight dropping along the groove in the sash,
glass rattling in the frame? Or suppose
it is a man, coughing in the other room,
the rasp of his throat sawing through
the thin wall, there, just above the mirror?
Or suppose it is a telephone ringing
from the house next door, and the blur
of bird wings crosses silently through it?
Or an engine overhead, riding unevenly
in thick clouds, a steady hum coming on
so gradually? Suppose you fail to hear it?
Suppose it is as unportentous as that?

What You Wanted

And when you finally find what you want,
they say, please allow six to eight weeks
for delivery, and then while you are waiting
you forget what you ordered or decide that
after all you could have lived without it.

When it comes, you leave it unopened
in the front hall for months.
It gathers dust and gets in the way,
but after a certain amount of time
it is far too late to send it back.

Reluctantly, you start to open it.
Somehow you manage to get one of the staples
stuck deep in your thumb; it draws a tunnel
of purple-blue blood up to the wound.
It hurts—a lot. You need a knife

to cut through the tape over the box flaps,
and as you sink the blade in
you feel like a hapless magician, hoping
that those who planned this magic trick
knew exactly what they were doing.

A Kind of Deliverance

Now my life opens, as suddenly
as the green that blurs across
the land in April, prodigious
as a magnolia flower, emerging
from the wand of the magic branch.

I will not say this season is
without its own blend of cruelty,
bred out of countless dead fields,
out of that bare ruined choir
of the year. I will say

it comes on inexorably, like a
child descending the birth canal,
pushed forward by contracting circles
of muscle, molding the mother's
bone and skin to her swift passage.

And who can tell which body is
most helpless: whether it is the
small one, forced out of a warm
ocean where she was rocked in the
constant beat of her mother's heart,

or whether it is the body that
felt the auger at work in her womb,
the nauseous wave as the cells divided
and spun themselves into fingerbuds and
the tiny black speck of an eye, when

after many months, she imagined
that this occupation would last forever,
that she would always have those tiny feet
dancing the walls of her belly, and that birth
would not come along with its fistful of keys.

In Quest of Agates

And I have walked on golden graveled roads
my head bent in search of the red agate,
alert for a pockmarked skin or the ripple
of ringed color split wide open. My feet scraped
out movement, my head swung from side to side,
sweeping, sifting through the ordinary limestone,
the white quartz, the granite shards—all the
rocky way that was not the glorious, elusive agate.

And I have heard the sound of meadowlarks as
I walked, the song of the field arising from
the plowey black furrows, the fence posts
graying into the new spring grass. Moving
along my row with a planter's straight aim,
I have had time to see the red of willow wands,
the garter snake sunning on the rock, the boot print
in the soft ground along the edge of the road.

Poised above a summer's night, I have learned
to fall into the wingless body of sleep,
the sound of pebbles rattling in my joints,
my pockets filled with a stone-smooth heaviness.
I think to myself as I am drifting that
there are few people who find treasure in the road
without stumbling, without falling to their knees.

Living in the Body

Body is something you need in order to stay
on this planet, and you only get one.
And no matter which one you get, it will not
be satisfactory. It will not be beautiful
enough, it will not be fast enough, it will
not keep on for days at a time but will
pull you down into a sleepy swamp and
demand apples and coffee and chocolate cake.

Body is a thing you have to carry
from one day into the next. Always the
same eyebrows over the same eyes in the same
skin when you look in the mirror, and the
same creaky knee when you get up from the
floor and the same wrist under the watchband.
The changes you can make are small and
costly—better to leave it as it is.

Body is a thing that you have to leave
eventually. You know that because you have
seen others do it, others who were once like you,
living inside their pile of bones and
flesh, smiling at you, loving you,
leaning in the doorway, talking to you
for hours, and then one day they
are gone. No forwarding address.

Crossroads

The second half of my life will be black
to the white rind of the old and fading moon.
The second half of my life will be water
over the cracked floor of these desert years.
I will land on my feet this time,
knowing at least two languages and who
my friends are. I will dress for the
occasion, and my hair shall be
whatever color I please.
Everyone will go on celebrating the old
birthday, counting the years as usual,
but I will count myself new from this
inception, this imprint of my own desire.

The second half of my life will be swift,
past leaning fence posts, a gravel shoulder,
asphalt tickets, the beckon of open road.
The second half of my life will be wide-eyed,
fingers sifting through fine sands,
arms loose at my sides, wandering feet.
There will be new dreams every night,
and the drapes will never be closed.
I will toss my string of keys into a deep
well and old letters into the grate.

The second half of my life will be ice
breaking up on the river, rain
soaking the fields, a hand
held out, a fire,
and smoke going
upward, always up.

SELECTIONS FROM
COMING BACK TO THE BODY

Homesteading

Long ago, I settled on this piece of mind,
clearing a spot for memory, making a
road so that the future could come and go,
building a house of possibility.

I came across the prairie with only
my wagonload of words, fragile stories
packed in sawdust. I had to learn how
to press a thought like seed into the ground;

I had to learn to speak with a hammer,
how to hit the nail straight on. When
I took up the reins behind the plow,
I felt the land, threading through me,
stitching me into place.

Comforts of the Sun

To someone else these fields would be exotic:
the small rows of corn stretching straight
as lines of notebook paper, curving slightly over
the rise of a hill; the thick green

of the oat fields, which I could predict
would turn into the flat gold of summer straw;
the curled alfalfa, slung like a jacket
over the shoulder of horizon.

To someone else, the small groves of trees
along the barbed-wire fence would look like
shrines to a distant god, little remnants
of woodland standing against the tilling hand.

Someone else would need to be told
that my footprints, in a hundred different
sizes, are etched under layers of gray
silt at the center of the farmyard,

that bits of my father's skin are plowed
into every acre. They would have
to be told how I know each tree,
each rock too heavy to lift.

Girl on a Tractor

I knew the names of all the cows before
I knew my alphabet, but no matter the
subject; I had mastery of it, and when
it came time to help in the fields, I
learned to drive a tractor at just the right
speed, so that two men, walking
on either side of the moving wagon
could each lift a bale, walk toward
the steadily arriving platform and
simultaneously hoist the hay onto
the rack, walk to the next bale, lift,
turn, and find me there, exactly where
I should be, my hand on the throttle,
carefully measuring out the pace.

A Poem with My Mother in It

The problem is getting her into the poem
where she doesn't want to be anymore than
she wants to be in the photograph, hearing
her make that rueful threat (as she steps into
place) about broken cameras and ruined film.

Once she's in, the problem is keeping her
there, with her feet up, ankles above the
heart (doctor's orders). Picture her, hurrying
down a street with a string of kids behind her,
all of them running to keep up.

It's the late fifties and we've just spent
an eternity in the dentist's office.
The downtown stores blur by: Kresges,
J.C. Penney, Samson Shoes, Woolworth's.
Let's get this show on the road! she says.

The problem is knowing how to say this
without using what she taught us to avoid:
sentiment and gush, words too sweet to
digest. Now (sometimes) I can find a
Mother's Day card plain enough to please her:

One not edged with lace, not stacked with
rhyme. On the cover, there's a woman
in a garden where tomatoes ripen, eggplants
turn their purple shoulder to the sun, parsley
greens under the blue sky.

She walks into sweet corn so tall
that it swallows her up. Mom, I yell,
come out! I can't see you anymore.
Take it! she says. It'll be the best
picture of me you've ever seen.

Apple Season

The kitchen is sweet with the smell of apples,
big yellow pie apples, light in the hand,
their skins freckled, the stems knobby
and thick with bark, as if the tree
could not bear to let the apple go.
Baskets of apples circle the back door,
fill the porch, cover the kitchen table.

My mother and my grandmother are
running the apple brigade. My mother,
always better with machines, is standing
at the apple peeler; my grandmother,
more at home with a paring knife,
faces her across the breadboard.
My mother takes an apple in her hand,

She pushes it neatly onto the sharp
prong and turns the handle that turns
the apple that swivels the blade pressed
tight against the apple's side and peels
the skin away in long curling strips that
twist and fall to a bucket on the floor.
The apples, coming off the peeler,

Are winding staircases, little accordions,
slinky toys, jack-in-the-box fruit, until
my grandmother's paring knife goes slicing
through the rings and they become apple
pies, apple cakes, apple crisp. Soon
they will be married to butter and live with
cinnamon and sugar, happily ever after.

Fields in Late October

The fields have turned their backs
to the cooling sun. They have gathered
the yellow stubble of summer and taken it
under the hills for the mice to eat.

Do not tell me how this turning happened.
I know it was the plow with its sharp claw
that ripped away the ripened skin. I know
the tractor roared each furrow into being.

Still I know the fields have turned
away from greening and from gazing
hopefully at the promise of a fickle sky.
The fields are through with growing.

It no longer matters to them what clouds
gather on the horizon, or what rain
is suspended over them like love,
something that never falls until too late.

The fields are sleeping. Do not disturb them.
Move quietly about your wintry business.

Casino

My mind is shuffling its deck tonight,
slipping one card over another,
letting them fall together at the corners,
the random hand of memory
is dealing from the bottom of the pack.

First: a bearded man emptying
the dragon kiln, then a woman
whistling, her face turned away
as she opens the oven. Next:
a big cat, six toes on each paw,
climbing up the yard pole. Last:
a pair of workhorses circling a tree
until they grind themselves to dust.

There is no one home in the world
tonight. Everyone is out of range.
The cradles are empty, the boughs
broken down. Trees go helter-skelter
and the wheel is creaking on its shaft.
Hit me, I say to the dealer. Hit me again.

Of Virtue

Assuming a virtue
if I had it not, I assumed
that virtue would find me,
which it did, and found me lacking,
and lacking it, I had to assume
that my pretense at virtue
was over, that use would never
change the stamp of nature, that
nature would not be changed by
using virtue as a customary thing.

Custom, however, meant
little to me, consisting only
in that I never wanted to make
the same move twice. I was ruined
from the start, born under
the hottest August sky, the
shimmer of summer on the
horizon, the loosened link
between green and ripe,
waters inviting but forbidden,
dog days slipping the leash.

The Silence Says

The silence says use your eyes now.
A leaf is just a manifestation of green,
a leaf has its own geometry.
What is the theorem for basswood?
What is the maple leaf's proof?

The silence says the beating in your wrist
is the rhythm you are always listening for
in the tabor and drums, in a blues note bending.
What is the time signature of loneliness?
What is that syncopated joy?

The silence hints that it has more to say,
it wants to ask you out to dinner,
or spend the weekend with you.
It needs you, is pointing a finger
in your direction, hoping to be irresistible.

It says these things in other languages;
it hisses, fills up with static, and sometimes it
goes off the air, leaving a long trail of quiet,
clean as newly braided rope and useful for
what it pulls behind, what it ties together.

A Kind of Villanelle

I will have been walking away:
no matter what direction I intended,
at that moment, I will have been walking

Away into the direction that you now say
I have always intended, no matter what my
intention was then, I will have been

Walking away, though it will not be clear
what it was that I was leaving or
even why, it seems that you will say

That always, I was walking away,
intending a direction that was not toward
you, but moving away with every step,

Or, even when I pretended to be walking
toward you, only making the place
for my feet to go backward,

Away, where I will have been walking,
always away: intention and direction
unknown, but knowing you will always
say I will have been walking away.

Her Legendary Head

This is the way the woman in
a Picasso painting feels, with her
mobile nose holding two eyes
to one side, her quivering lip
ascending into a pointed chin.

The world is now (and she
can hear its roar) all a blood-
dimmed tide, things fall
apart and then together, banged
and whimpering they begin.

All her life, she was up to
her neck in marble, and
the gyres in her head. Just
another woman in pieces,
inventory lost, instructions

too small to read. Broken
the lines of her, a memorially
reconstructed version, awaiting
the detection of each separate
and mysterious error.

Not for Burning

I come across your old letters,
the words still clinging to the page,
holding onto their places patiently,
with no intention of abandoning
the white spaces. They say
that you will always love me,
and reading them again, I almost
believe it, but I suspect that
they are heretics, that later,
in the fire, they will deny it all.

Then I remember something I once
read (my memory is filled with voices
of the dead): that "it is an heretic that
makes the fire," and that I am more guilty
than your words, poor pilgrims who trusted
the road you sent them down, and kept
severely to the way. I forgive them;
I let them live to proclaim freely what
they thought would always be true.

The Temptation to Invent

It is very strong,
especially when the memory is hazy.

It begins with "I once knew a man,"
and ends with "but it didn't work out."

I always remember something more substantial
than the details, something that does not translate.

Most of what I know is contagious. I
caught it from reading books and passed it on.

But tenderness has disappeared from my tongue;
parts of my heart are missing.

I realize that plot is not essential,
but I get tired of just words, words, words.

Reflecting is simply my way of turning away
from the past. What you see is no longer happening.

Bookmobile

I spend part of my childhood waiting
for the Stearns County Bookmobile.
When it comes to town, it makes a
U-turn in front of the grade school and
glides into its place under the elms.

It is a natural wonder of late
afternoon. I try to imagine Dante,
William Faulkner, and Emily Dickinson
traveling down a double lane highway
together, country-western on the radio.

Even when it arrives, I have to wait.
The librarian is busy, getting out
the inky pad and the lined cards.
I pace back and forth in the line,
hungry for the fresh bread of the page,

Because I need something that will tell me
what I am; I want to catch a book,
clear as a one-way ticket, to Paris,
to London, to anywhere.

Rodin on Film

Rodin is at the top of the stairs
like a sculpted man. He stands still
until, on command, he comes down,
down, down, as if descending a throne.

Pygmalion-like, he is thinking of
flesh, of flesh turning to stone, stone
turning to bone, moment without
movement, marble into motion.

Rodin works his hammer and
chisel, blinks away stone with a
flickering eye, and steps back
(rough-flaked with marble)

to turn the torso on its wooden
pedestal, wedge his chisel, strike,
turn it again and strike another
blow. He does these things for

the camera; he already knows how
it will work: how it will make his
body into flat dead air and then
let it pretend it is heavy with life.

Arrangement in Grey and Black

I wonder how the artist got
his mother to hold still
long enough for him to paint her.

Wasn't she constantly getting up
to bring him a cup of tea?
to find the brush he needed?

Didn't she tell him at least
a dozen times that no one would
want to look at an old woman?

At last, he turned her sideways
and told her to look out the window
while he painted her profile.

The sky was deepest blue,
and the clouds went over the horizon
like salmon, leaping up a golden stair.

"Oh Jimmy," she whispered, but
did not move, only her glance
brightening beneath the darkened brows.

What the Heart Cannot Forget

Everything remembers something. The rock, its fiery bed,
cooling and fissuring into cracked pieces, the rub
of watery fingers along its edge.

The cloud remembers being elephant, camel, giraffe,
remembers being a veil over the face of the sun,
gathering itself together for the fall.

The turtle remembers the sea, sliding over and under
its belly, remembers legs like wings, escaping down
the sand under the beaks of savage birds.

The tree remembers the story of each ring, the years
of drought, the floods, the way things came
walking slowly toward it long ago.

And the skin remembers its scars, and the bone aches
where it was broken. The feet remember the dance,
and the arms remember lifting up the child.

The heart remembers everything it loved and gave away,
everything it lost and found again, and everyone
it loved the heart cannot forget.

Older, Younger, Both

I feel older, younger, both
at once. Every time I win,
I lose. Every time I count,
I forget and must begin again.

I must begin again, and again I
must begin. Every time I lose,
I win and must begin again.

Everything I plan must wait and
having to wait has made me old and
the older I get, the more I wait, and everything
I'm waiting for has already been planned.

I feel sadder, wiser, neither
together. Everything is almost
true, and almost true is everywhere.
I feel sadder, wiser, neither at once.

I end in beginning, in ending I find
that beginning is the first thing to do.
I stop when I start, but my heart keeps on beating
so I must go on starting in spite of the stopping.

I must stop my stopping and start to start—
I can end at the beginning or begin at the end.
I feel older, younger, both at once.

Coming Back to the Body

Coming back to the body, as if to
a house abandoned in time of war, you find
it stands as tall as you left it, the same
fingers reaching back to rub the same neck.

Returning, you remember how it feels
to stretch your arms to embrace another
body, how the tongue clicks against the teeth,
how solid voices flow into your ear.

You are relieved that what you dreamed will not
come true now that you have escaped again
into skin and bone. They'll never think of
looking for you in the body, alive.

Wherever the body is that's where you
are now. It's the same old address you had
before you went away; no miracles,
no amazing improvements. You're still you.

Now that you are back, things go on the way
they were meant to. No one asks the question
that you couldn't answer if you wanted:
Where were you hiding all those long lost years?

Into Thin Air

The expense of spirit is, in fact, what
I worry about. Not so much the body,
dragging itself from limb to limb,
falling helplessly down the vast
recesses of night, hanging between
dream and the uneven ticking of clocks.

Not so much even the eyes failing, light
spent, especially when I consider Degas,
who had the weakest eyes in Paris,
still managed to draw a black line around
the body, shoulders edged with a perfection
no one else, seeing better, could ever find.

But who is it, I wonder, who also serves?
And what is it to only stand and wait?
O body swayed and brightening glance,
cast off that waste of shame, and think
(beating mind!) of how it will be to fade
into thin air! What expense of spirit!

The Assumption

That would be the way to go:
straight up on a cloud,
the crowd below craning
their necks as you disappeared
out of view and then
the wondering: which cloud
overhead was under you.

There would be no dying then
for you, you would be one of
the seldom few, who did not need
to disembark but kept her place
as the boat went over the waterfall,
as the camel passed through
the eye of the needle,

as the soldiers searched the train.
And what made you so lucky? What
had you ever done to deserve this
favor? Nothing, not one thing. No
immaculate conception, no swing
low sweet chariot, no friendship with
an angel. You just assumed that it

would happen this way, that
all the practice shots, the dress
rehearsals, the final countdown,
none of it mattered. You assumed
that you would be lifted up, up, and
away—and you were, oh yes, you were.

SELECTIONS FROM *NAMING THE STARS*

Naming the Stars

This present tragedy will eventually
turn into myth, and in the mist
of that later telling the bell tolling
now will be a symbol, or, at least,
a sign of something long since lost.

This will be another one of those
loose changes, the rearrangement of
hearts, just parts of old lives
patched together, gathered into
a dim constellation, small consolation.

Look, we will say, you can almost see
the outline there: her fingertips
touching his, the faint fusion
of two bodies breaking into light.

Raku Songs

I

He never dated them, but he put what
part of the week it was and gave the time
of day—as in "Thursday, early evening,"
or "Friday, morning," so that when
she read them again how much easier
it was to think that then could be now
and what he said might still be true.

Of the weather, he always had something
to say. Once, in early spring when
the ice melted and then froze again,
he walked on a pond and watched
mud and water ooze under his feet
until the soft ice broke. It was shallow
there, he said, and barely covered his shoes.

II

Intended: one letter,
written in the sun
of the marina, palm trees
and parrots (yellow and green)
squawking overhead
while he watched
sails filling in the breeze,
sending her his letter,
which would cover her
with a fine tropic mist.

Instead: something
he wrote as he
looked out the window
at sparrows
pecking in the dirt.

III

He begins in the kitchen,
but ends up in the library.
First it was a drink, calling
him in, then the need for nuts and bolts.
When he thinks about writing, he sees
pages and pages ahead, scenes moving
by like liquid wallpaper. He dips
his pen in and sends her a small cup.

On the back of the page, he daydreams
in fine-lined designs: spaceships
circling in silent concentration, avoiding
touch, no possibility of collision up there.
Momentum evades me, he says, and then:
No, I evade *it*, until time is short.

IV

Monday—no, Tuesday—this one begins.
He's writing on cream-colored cards,
small ones, no real paper to be found,
but he has a new pen.

With his new pen, he says he loves
her; he imagines walking with her when
she is walking in silence and wonders
what she will say when she begins to speak.

When he walks the neighbor's dog, they both
miss her, he says, and then he comes to the end
of the cards, writes "Goodbye for a while"
and "Love," in tiny letters above his name.

V

He tells her that each word is
surrounded by others that don't
get written. I should be putting down
colors instead, he says, or stoking up
fires, in five different shades. Against
her wishes, he sends a present:
a bird guide, slightly used. Imagine me
paging through it in a school van.
The letter, this time, is on parchment
and crinkles when she folds it,
but the pages of the book are soft
as that bird who unrolled his feathers
and rowed him softly home, or butterflies.
He knew she would see him in it
and know he saw her seeing him in
every word he wrote, every bird she saw.

How We Ended Up Together

He was good in an emergency, calm
in the middle of a storm. Accidents
didn't surprise him; he was always

ready for whatever came along. You
could count on him; you could make
a deal and he would keep it, even if you

couldn't. His deals were impossible;
his deals were meant to make you fail,
and failing you found yourself in some

sort of emergency, someplace you didn't
want to be, and he was good at getting
you back to the ground, back to your feet.

I chose him for what he could not give me,
and he chose me because I would not ask
until I was desperate and only he could help.

The Problem Was

The problem was a different sense of form.
He was all couplets, heroic and closed;
I always wanted to carry on, one line
into the next, never reaching an end,
or, if I did, imagining it might be
the possible beginning to a different train
of thought, which might lead to the exact
opposite of what I was saying now.

The problem was we rhymed in various ways:
he liked perfection; I preferred the wise
conjunction of nearly alike, almost
a match made in heaven, both of us most
certain we knew where to take the next line.
He loved his words the best, and I loved mine.

Losing Touch

As if I had died, you heard nothing
from me after that day, and if you thought
about me at times I never knew.

We went on living our missing lives
as if there were centuries between us.
We could have been on different planets,

except that we weren't, and it was
the same moon (more or less) rising over
(more or less) the same world.

The news happened, and we heard it
together, watching identical faces in
different rooms. Once or twice we probably

passed each other on the freeway or
in the airport. There was a moment of hesitation
before we went on, as if someone had died.

Polaroid # 2

You took this picture of me;
because of that I can see how
I once looked to you.

You stood with the lake
behind you and put a frame
around me. Smile, you said.

I can't remember how it felt
to look the way I do
in the picture, but I can

remember how it felt to look
out from that body to where
you stood, telling me to smile.

I'm always smiling in this picture,
but no matter how hard I look,
I can't see to where you're standing,

watching this picture of me come
out of the darkness, holding
that one day in your hand.

Ever After

What am I to you now that you are no
longer what you used to be to me?

Who are we to each other now that
there is no us, now that what we once

were is divided into me and you
who are not one but two separate and

unrelated persons except for that ex-
that goes in front of the words

that used to mean me, used to mean
you, words we rarely used (husband, wife)

as when we once posed (so young and helpless)
with our hands (yours, mine) clasped on the knife

that was sinking into the tall white cake.
All that sweetness, the layers of one thing

and then another, and then one thing again.

The Sound of No One Calling

The sound of no one calling is a car
approaching and then heading into
the distance. It's the dishwasher
going through its cycles, one
click at a time, a squirrel chattering
in the tree outside the window.

The sound of no one calling is
empty shelves, the scrape of
the scoop at the bottom of the bin.
It's the faint light of the moon
through a cloudy veil, the ocean
inside a shell you hold up to your ear,
each time pretending to hear more.

It's rain on a tin roof—or a window
rattling in the wind, a needle drifting
aimlessly over the tractless vinyl
spinning on the turntable.
It's the furnace kicking in, the house
creaking, the clock, finally, ticking.

Aisle and View

Sometimes I was so lonely
that I liked grocery shopping.
I made it take a long time
and got every single thing
on the list. It wasn't important
to talk to anyone; I simply liked
the camaraderie of being
one body among others,
looking at the cake mixes.

I lingered in certain sections.
The spice aisle was educational,
and it always cheered me up
to read what the labels said.
There were commands: "Use
in barbecue sauce," "Rub
into steak prior to cooking,"
"Add zip to any salad," and
there were descriptions: "From
India, its earthy flavor is featured
in many Middle Eastern and
Latin American foods." I wished
I was from India and "earthy."

For hours (days, months, years!)
I wandered under the high
fluorescent lights (Oh Philip Larkin!
What thoughts I had of you
among those sad shelves stacked
with cereal and sugar as white
as the lost light of distant stars!).

The Apostate's Creed

My fingers fumble on the keys;
I am caught between the pages.
In my dream I cut off my hair, then try
to put it back again. Life is crooked.

There is always one thing I need,
one thing missing, one thing I never
expected. Snow begins to fall and
falls all through the night. I wake, and

everything has been canceled. I love
the world when it is white, right after
the snow stops and the skies turn blue,
when there are no footprints.

Whatever is right was wrong once.
Do not say that this temple was built by
prayer or that church rose on a song;
there was blood, and gold changed hands.

Empty

I wanted so badly to be good.
I wanted everything to turn out right
in the end. I wanted to go to heaven.

Whatever I thought I should lose,
I lost; whatever the cost,
I paid it. Nothing was too much.

I worked hard at letting go; I
learned the art of denial. Wine
turned into water, bread to stone.

I was the bone singing in the desert,
the gate swinging on its hinge;
I was the bell ringing and ringing.

What Comes After

Repentance is not enough; forgiveness
is required, but you can only make a request,
then wait to see what happens. What you leave
at the doorstep, the letters that you send,
the many ways you try to repair the shame—
all of these things are better for the soul
than repentance, which is only one more
way of saying you would do it again.

When you ask to be forgiven, you must
not expect punishment without revenge;
there is no such thing as being even.
One day you may find that your offering
has been accepted, and the next day
you could be walking through the gate, almost
as if you were a prodigal coming
home to find that all has been forgiven.

In the Wake

Everything I saved from the flood
went into the fire: one thing to keep
me warm, another because it
was old and useless, and one
just for the burning.

I had dreams, forgotten in the morning
as I dressed and got on with my life.
If I had it to do over again,
I would do nothing
the same.

Now that it's over, I don't know what
to make instead of a prayer. Now
the roof's gone, I can't
hear the sound of
the rain.

This Body

When I stepped ashore in this body
I was recognized at once
and given a name.

My bones were smaller, but the shape
of the cheek and the chin
are the same.

This is the only body I know: this color
my eyes, this color my skin.
Every scar is mine.

I have become as tall, as slim, as old
as I am. My voice has carried the weight
of what I had to say,

Words were scattered along the way: words
on gravel roads, in hallways and staircases.
Words on a wire.

Somewhere in a field, my hair. Somewhere in a lake,
my skin, some rooftop where my gaze rested,
some star, a wish.

This is my address on earth: temporary, fragile,
a name in the phone book,
at the moment alive.

Now That Anything Could Happen

You now know that anything could happen;
things that never happened before, things that
only happened in movies and nightmares
are happening now, as if nothing could
stop them. You know now that you are not safe,
you know you live in fragile skin and bones,
that even steel and concrete can melt away,
and that the earth itself can come unhinged,
shaken from its orbit around the sun.
You know, now that anything can happen,
it's hard to know what will, and what will you
do now that you know? What words will you say
now that you could say anything? What hands
will you hold? Whose heart will beat inside you?

What to Pack

Either nothing you've ever worn before
or everything old and warm. Only
one of anything, but bring along all

of something. Don't forget a few worthless
items so you can leave what you really
need at home. Pack lightly and pack often;

practice packing in the middle of night.
Before you fall asleep, picture the trip
you have always wanted to take and pack

the things you'll need there: a lute, a pear tree,
and a dove the color of a cloud packed
with thousands of raindrops, each one of them

standing at the open door in the sky
with a ticket and a tiny suitcase.

Getting the Machine

It was good to hear
my own voice again
when I called, after
being gone for weeks.
I sounded about the same.
I hadn't changed my name;
didn't have a foreign accent.
I just said I couldn't
come to the phone right then,
exactly the way I'd been
saying it for years,
and so I left myself
a little message
saying how sorry
I was I wasn't there,
and that I'd be
home soon. I tried to
think of what I'd want
to hear myself saying
and say it right.

Some Glad Morning

One day, something very old
happened again. The green
came back to the branches,
settling like leafy birds
on the highest twigs;
the ground broke open
as dark as coffee beans.

The clouds took up their
positions in the deep stadium
of the sky, gloving the
bright orb of the sun
before they pitched it
over the horizon.

It was as good as ever:
the air was filled
with the scent of lilacs
and cherry blossoms
sounded their long
whistle down the track.
It was some glad morning.

At the Moment

Suddenly, I stopped thinking about Love,
after so many years of only that,
after thinking that nothing else mattered.

And what was I thinking of when I stopped
thinking about Love? Death, of course—what else
could take Love's place? What else could hold such force?

I thought about how far away Death once
had seemed, how unexpected that it could
happen to someone that I knew quite well,

how impossible that this should be the
normal thing, as natural as frost and
winter. I thought about the way we'd aged,

how skin fell into wrinkles, how eyes grew
dim; then (of course) my love, I thought of you.

Now, Finally, a Love Song

Now, finally, I'll write you a love song,
or, at least, something that we're both
in, saying things that I should have said long
ago, and you'll be happy to hear them.

Now finally, I'll say what a wonder
you are, and you'll wonder why I never
told you that before, and I'll ask whether
we could make a life together under

the circumstances, which seem to have changed
since yesterday and every day since
we met each other long ago, distance
hard to measure, two lives rearranged.

And finally, I know what we should do:
I know the song; I'll sing it to you.

SELECTIONS FROM *FIRST WORDS*

First Words

My father and mother must have said
many things, because I had to learn all
my first words from them—no television,

no day care—just a man and a woman
in the circle that makes a farm—
house and barn, shop and granary,

chicken coop, silos, machine shed,
and corn crib. My grandparents had built
a house in town, but they came back

with their own words and their voices
slipped into the ones I was learning—
cow, chicken, dog, pig, and horse,

tractor, fences, rhubarb, please, and
thank you. Lilacs. I must have listened to
the radio with its livestock reports

and polkas—and then on Sundays
there was Latin—*Introibo
ad altare Dei*, which I did not

understand, anymore than I did
the milk machine pumping like
a heart to draw down the warm milk.

The Body I Once Lived In

The body I once lived in was smaller.
It stood at the top of the stairs and waved
good night; it wore pajamas that had feet.

That body could swing on ropes in the hay barn
and run alongside wagons in the field.
That one loved to eat pancakes and sausages.

The body I once lived in sucked her thumb
and had nightmares about rattlesnakes and pigs.
Next day, the rooster crowed, the sun came up,

And the body I once lived in walked out
over the dewy grass to let the cows
into the barn, stood in the aisle watching

Until a head was in each place, then closed
the stanchions one by one and brought the milkers
in. That body did not look in mirrors.

That one never wore shoes in summer,
except on Sundays, only took a bath
on Saturdays, wore whatever clothes fit.

My Legendary Father

Here are some other things he could do: he
could weld old water pipes into a swing;
he could build a mountain out of snow; he

could lay a field of hay flat, then twist it
into long green ribbons and pack it up
into bales for winter; he could squirt a

stream of milk into a kitten's open
"meow"; he could carry four roosters at
once, all of them swinging upside down, their

yellow feet gathered like kindling in his
big hands; he could ride a horse bareback, no
bridle, and on Sundays he could be our

eternal pitcher, sending one perfect
strike after another over home plate.

The Kingdom of Summer

In my mother's cellar there were
realms of golden apple, rooms
of purple beet, hallways of green bean
leading to windows of
strawberry and grape.

In her cellar there were
cider seas and
pumpkin shores,
mountains of tomatoes—
pickle trees.

When I walked down the steps
and pulled on the light,
I saw where she kept the
Kingdom of Summer.

The Aunts

I like it when they get together
and talk in voices that sound
like apple trees and grapevines,

and some of them wear hats
and go to Arizona in the winter,
and they all like to play cards.

They will always be the ones
who say "It is time to go now,"
even as we linger at the door,

or stand by the waiting cars, they
remember someone—an uncle we
never knew—and sigh, all

of them together, like wind
in the oak trees behind the farm
where they grew up—a place

I remember—especially
the henhouse and the soft
clucking that filled the sunlit yard.

My Luck

When I was five, my father,
who loved me, ran me over
with a medium-sized farm tractor.

I was lucky though; I tripped
and slipped into a small depression,
which caused the wheels to tread

lightly on my leg, which had already
been broken (when I was three)
by a big dog, who liked to play rough,

and when I was eight, I fell
from the second-floor balcony
onto the cement by the back steps,

and as I went down I saw my life go by
and thought: "This is exactly how
Wiley Coyote feels, every time!"

Luckily, I mostly landed on my feet,
and only had to go on crutches
for a few months in the fifth grade—

and shortly after that, my father,
against his better judgment,
bought the horse I'd wanted for so long.

All the rest of my luck has to do
with highways and ice—things that
could have happened, but didn't.

Just for the Record

It wasn't like that. Don't imagine
my father in a feed cap, chewing
a stem of alfalfa, spitting occasionally.

No bib overalls over bare shoulders,
no handkerchief around his neck.
Don't imagine he didn't shave every morning.

The buildings on his farm weren't
weathered gray; the lawns were always mowed.
Don't imagine a car in the weeds.

I tell you this because you have certain
ideas about me, about farmers
and their daughters.

You imagine him bumbling along, some
hayseed, when really, he wore his dark
suit as gracefully as Cary Grant.

The one thing you're right about
is that he worked too hard. You can't
imagine how early and how late.

Bringing in the Hay

There must have been a dozen other times
when we finished making hay just before

the skies opened, but I remember best
the time that I rode home on the wagon,

looking back at the bare hayfield, pointing
to the clouds gathered in the west (angry

thunderheads, forking streaks of lightning)
and saw the fingered tunnel descending.

Something was up in the sky, bellying
down over our fields, and I could see how

we looked from above: a man on a red
tractor pulling a wagonload of hay,

a girl sitting on the top bale calling
to the black-and-white dog that trailed behind.

The beast surveyed the scene, and then because
we were meant to live, moved on to the east.

We had the hay in the barn, and supper
was on the table when the rains came down.

My Dog, Pal

Once, in the yellow glow of the hay barn,
my father and I met a stray, and that dog
stayed and lived with us a while.

I named him "Pal" because he was friendly
and reminded me of a storybook dog.
Even now I can see him sitting

at my feet, his head tipped slightly to one
side, his shoulders squared back against
the passing of another boring day.

Thin and houndy, he was made for wilder
things than fetching sticks and shaking hands with
six-year-olds. I think he was a hobo dog,

and one day he was gone, without
a backward glance; his house, his dish, his supper
bone—nothing there to tie him down.

Harrow

I want to praise
the harrow,
first for its name,
which when I write it,

is like unto what it is,
and that (as I remember)
is a collection of iron points
held together by
a wide and wooden frame.

Nothing about
the harrow is harrowing—
leave that to the mower
or the combine.

The harrow comes
after the disk, which comes
after the plow. The plow
was yesterday; the harrow
is now.

For the harrow rides
over the field, it moves
like a stream over rock,
like rain on the roof.

For when the world
is turned inside
out, the harrow
slips it back into
its skin again.

The Oat Binder

First, I had to explain an oat field
and how it is green, then gold—
waves of it, like wheat, but with
a different kind of head, and how the
oat binder cut down the ripened oats
with its sideways sharp teeth and let
them fall flat onto the canvas platform,
then carried them along under the wooden
wings turning like paddle wheels on
a riverboat, gathered it into bundles,
and then—through some crafty sleight of
its mechanical hand—tied up the bundle
and dropped it back to the stubbled field.

Then I had to explain how we came
walking through the field to set the bundles
together like this: three pairs, head to head,
and one pulled over the top, like a hat
(we called this "shocking the oats"), and then
I had to tell about the threshing machine,
how it was as big as houses and how
it lumbered down the hill behind the county's
oldest tractor like a tamed behemoth,
and how its handlers—Harold and Elmer—
were missing parts of their arms and legs.

But I didn't tell about the wagons, the
pitchforks, and the tractor standing back,
attached to a long belt that turned wheels that
turned the wheels on the threshing machine,
and if you touched that belt it was like
touching fire, and I didn't say anything
about the pickup trucks waiting to receive
the oats and carry them back to the granaries.

But I did talk about the straw, as it fell
like Rapunzel's hair into a yellow heap,
but then I had to explain straw, how it
was beautifully flat and smooth (not stiff
and scratchy like hay, not something cows ate)
and how we shook it out under the cows
as they swished their tails in the warm barn,
while the snow gathered in drifts all around.

And I explained about the men in the
threshing crew and how they worked from
farm to farm, dawn to dusk, only stopping
at noon to wash their blackened hands
and devour plates filled with meat and mashed
potatoes, gravy, dressing, three kinds of
vegetables, stacks of bread with butter and
jam, pickles, applesauce, and then (of
course) pie and coffee. I suppose I mentioned
(again) how I helped in the fields until
I had to help in the kitchen and how
I hated being the girl who filled the
water glasses and served the pies, staying
behind to do the dishes before I could
go back to the fields, but it wasn't worth
complaining now to someone who never
saw an oat binder—or a threshing machine
or a horse in harness—and who couldn't
tell a handful of alfalfa from oat straw
and who probably never climbed a silo.

I couldn't decide if I felt lucky or not.
What I really wanted to tell you, I said,
was how we used to play on the oat binder
at the back of the machine shed and that
the light fell into place, like ripened oats.
What I really wanted to tell you was that

the oat binder was as beautiful as
a ship under sail, that it took its sweet
time with the field and left all of the gold
for us. What I really wanted to say
is that I know (yes) how lucky I've been.

"H"

Of all tractors, I love the "H" the best:
first for its proportions, the ratio of body to machine,
arm to wheel, leg to clutch, hand to throttle,

and for the way it does not drown the voice,
but forces it to rise above the engine,
and for the smoke signaling from the silver pipe,

for the rip-rap of tread on the big tires, driver
perched between them, as on a throne in kingdoms of oats
and corn, scrolling along the meadow's edge,

then sometimes standing still, engine turning the belt
that turned the wheels in the hammer mill
or whirling the gears that divided the oats from the straw.

And "H" for the ache to see my father plowing fields again—
the silhouette of a red tractor and a man, one hand
on the wheel, the other waving free.

What Every Girl Wants

I wanted a horse. This was long after
we sold the work horses, and I was feeling

restless on the farm. I got up early
to help my father milk the cows, talking

a blue streak about TV cowboys
he never had time to see and trying to

convince him that a horse wouldn't cost
so much and that I'd do all the work.

He listened while he leaned his head
against the flank of a Holstein, pulling

the last line of warm milk into
the stainless bucket. He kept listening

while the milk machine pumped like an engine,
and the black-and-silver cups fell off and

dangled down, clanging like bells when he
stepped away, balancing the heavy milker

against the vacuum hose and the leather belt.
I knew he didn't want the trouble

of a horse, but I also knew there was nothing
else I wanted the way I wanted a horse—

another way of saying I wanted
to ride into the sunset and (maybe)

never come back—I think he knew that too.
We'll see, he said, we'll see what we can do.

The First Child
(for Sarah)

It is hard to be the first,
the one who opens the door
between generations, who
swings between the mother
and the father, the one who
must learn to sleep through
the night, alone.

    The oldest one,
the eldest, the one who
has her first birthday first
and her second birthday
first, and first rides a bike,
and first goes off to school
and has her picture taken
a hundred times a day.

The first one makes mistakes
that show the others what
to avoid. She must go down
into the dark underworld
of parental ignorance and come
up with a key that will
release her and her sisters
from the fortress where
the ogres planned to keep them
all their lives.

    She has to be
the first to tell them no, make
them let go. She has to tell them
she isn't going to be a virtuoso,
doesn't want straight As, won't
take accelerated math, has to

find her own way. First to say
love me for who I am.
First to want the car keys, first
to hit a tree, first to stay out
late, first not to come home
at all. She makes them pace
the floor, believing in the aliens
that take the real child and leave
heavy metal in her place.

    But she's
the first to come back home,
first to remember your birthday
and Mother's Day, a bit
extravagant, as first-borns
tend to be. She begins
to admire the way you arrange
your furniture, pages through
your books, notices the
colors in your kitchen—
and then one day she invites you
to dinner, and clearly
she has spent the whole day
making sure everything
is absolutely
perfect.

My Brother's Hat

And sometimes I am my brother
as I lift my chin to signal "No"
the way he learned to do in Turkey,

and sometimes when I slip my foot
into a shoe I think of the
red scorpions in the jungle

and of the giant rats under the cot
that kept falling apart in Paraguay
and of the piranhas.

And sometimes I dream in Spanish
or Guarani, but never in French because
I know enough to know better,

and I do not buy anything except for
parsley and scallions and other
things I need to make tabbouleh,

and also the ingredients
for the most delicious (and healthy)
cookies in the world,

and I am he in how I remember
another side of the story, the one
that I never tell, the part

I couldn't see, and, circling the lake,
wondering about the hawk
who dove down and took his hat,

I am he (days later) when it appears
in the branches of a tree, and there
I am, looking up at my hat.

These Few Precepts
(for Marna)

I said to her, don't leave your life
scattered in boxes across the country,

don't slip away without tying down
the hatch, don't walk a mile out of

your way to avoid a crack, don't
worry about breaking your mother's

back. I'm sorry, I said, that I was
stupid when I married; I'm sorry I

chose for right instead of love, for
truth instead of beauty. They aren't

always the same thing you know,
despite what Keats said. Don't try

to do it all alone, and if you fail,
think of how well you've failed

and how all you really need is a good
view of the sky or a bit of something

—a flower petal or speckled stone—
held close enough for the eye to

drink it in, and remember, I said,
I'll always love you, no matter what.

In Vermeer's Painting
(for Alicia)

In Vermeer's painting she turns
toward us, her head wrapped
in a blue and gold silk turban.
I know those eyes, the nose,

even the lips, parted with her
tongue light on the teeth,
the faint eyebrows, the shadow
and slope of the cheek, the chin.

Of course I'm amazed: what is
my daughter, now standing beside me,
doing in seventeenth century Holland?
Von Zutphen, I presume?

She looks pensive, as if the
pearl, floating above her robe
and collar, was indeed the pearl
of wisdom, but I know that

she is thinking about the future
when she will be born in
Lindbergh's town and how someday
she will dance on the moon.

She sees the centuries of pearl
the slow layering of generation
until this particular luster is
reached and stands now

in the museum, tilting her head
(first this way and then that)
to see what she's become:
in Vermeer's painting she turns.

Things You Didn't Put on Your Résumé

How often you got up in the middle of the night
when one of your children had a bad dream,

and sometimes you woke because you thought
you heard a cry but they were all sleeping,

so you stood in the moonlight just listening
to their breathing, and you didn't mention

that you were an expert at putting toothpaste
on tiny toothbrushes and bending down to wiggle

the toothbrush ten times on each tooth while
you sang the words to songs from *Annie,* and

who would suspect that you know the fingerings
to the songs in the first four books of the Suzuki

Violin Method and that you can do the voices
of Pooh and Piglet especially well, though

your absolute favorite thing to read out loud is
Bedtime for Frances and that you picked

up your way of reading it from Glynnis Johns,
and it is, now that you think of it, rather impressive

that you read all of Narnia and all of the Ring Trilogy
(and others too many to mention here) to them

before they went to bed and on the way out to
Yellowstone, which is another thing you don't put

on the résumé: how you took them to the ocean
and the mountains and brought them safely home.

How to Listen

Tilt your head slightly to one side and lift
your eyebrows expectantly. Ask questions.

Delve into the subject at hand or let
things come randomly. Don't expect answers.

Forget everything you've ever done.
Make no comparisons. Simply listen.

Listen with your eyes, as if the story
you are hearing is happening right now.

Listen without blinking, as if a move
might frighten the truth away forever.

Don't attempt to copy anything down.
Don't bring a camera or a recorder.

This is your chance to listen carefully.
Your whole life might depend on what you hear.

The Last Things I'll Remember

The partly open hay barn door, white frame around the darkness,
the broken board, small enough for a child
to slip through.

Walking in the cornfields in late July, green tassels overhead,
the slap of flat leaves as we pass, silent
and invisible from any road.

Hollyhocks leaning against the stucco house, peonies heavy
as fruit, drooping their deep heads
on the doghouse roof.

Lilac bushes between the lawn and the woods,
a tractor shifting from one gear into
the next, the throttle opened,

the smell of cut hay, rain coming across the river,
the drone of the hammer mill,
milk machines at dawn.

SELECTIONS FROM *AFTER WORDS*

A Dream of Empty Fields

As I read your words, I'm thinking along
with you, remembering a place I loved
the way you loved the place you are telling
me about. I know just what you mean here.

And when you say how it felt when you lost
that ground, how it was covered with cement
and brick and steel, I say I know how that
feels; I see houses where there once were fields,

street signs on corners that were open land,
stop signs to halt the traffic that began
as soon as they put a road through the field—
gas stations, grocery stores, everything.

Just once, I'd like to see them take it down,
pack up the houses, put away the town.

Taking Stock

Even when you couldn't see him
you knew he was standing
in the open door of the hay barn,
covered with a fine white powder of dust,
lifting gunny sacks of oats,
shoveling the dried ears of corn
into the wide throat of the hammer mill.

Later, in the barn below the hay barn,
he'd slide open the ground-feed chute,
let pour a gold dusty stream into
the basket propped on his knee,
then bump the tin bushel along
the top of the cement crib, measuring
each portion with a scoop, according to
some arcane calculation in pounds of milk
and butterfat. "It's like dessert to them,"
he said, meaning the cows.

II

He's always been a good dreamer,
the kind who could dream about the stars
bowing down to the earth or seven
fat cows devoured by seven lean cows.
He'd tell his dream
to anyone who wanted to hear it.
All week, after it happened,
he had the same dream:
he was smoothing a piece of wood,
sanding it down and seeing the grain,
clear as gravel washed in a stream,
so real, he said, you wanted to touch it,
rub your hand along its soft side.

III

If I try to hold him still,
I never can.
He's down in the meadow
cutting hay
and when he sees me waving,
he waves back,
big circles over his head, one arm
dancing free . . .
Mr. Bojangles.

Or he is hurrying from
one milk machine to another,
checking, adjusting, timing it
so that one by one,
he can finish milking each cow,
pull the vacuum hose from
the nozzle, unhook the milker
(and the long leather belt
that holds the milker in place),
step out from between cows,
hold the belt and hose up high
to balance
the steaming weight of the milker
as he walks to the milk can,
and pours a white-fall of fresh milk
into the stainless-steel strainer,
pauses, and then turns
to hook the empty milker
to another cow,
adjusting the belt, and then
leaping up to the next milker
(almost filled now) or pausing
to make an adjustment on

the one in between or the one
jangled by a cow who kicks
and tries to dance the milker
into the wall . . .

IV

Or I see him
getting onto his "H" tractor—
the way a cowboy in the old Westerns
mounts his horse—
and talking, waving, as he swings a leg
over the seat, settling his hands
on the wheel and throttle,
letting out the clutch
and galloping off.

Or maybe he's pulling away
with a wagon piled high with hay,
jumping down to open the gate,
leaping back up to drive through,
jumping down to close the gate,
leaping back to drive up the hill
to the wooden feeders he made last fall,
stopping at each one, lifting,
breaking open the bales with a thrust of his knee,
pulling back on the twine to spill
the chunks of hay into the feeder.

And sometimes he's at the gas pump,
as if he's brought his horse to water,
or sometimes he is arc welding in the shop,
menacing in his black welding mask,
until he stops for a minute, pushes up
the mask to say, "Look away now,"
and other times he's spraying apple-
blossoms in spring or digging potatoes
in fall, or pruning the grapevines

or piling wood in long piles, like cars
on a freight train that goes rolling by.
And sometimes he is sitting at the table,
the newspaper spread out in front of him,
coffee cup steaming at his elbow
and a minute later he's leaned back
in the chair, sleeping. . . .

V

It takes a long time, but finally
I begin asking the right questions
and I ask them more than once
until I know the answers by heart.

The Scythe

The scythe escaped the fire that burned the plow
and the oat-binder, that burned the baler
and the side rake, burned the cultivator,
the field chopper, the harrow, and the disk.

It was not hanging from a wall with the
hammers and the pliers; it was not on
the workbench with the anvil and the vice;
it wasn't on the hook above the door

or leaning against a wall with
the rake, the shovel, the sledgehammer, or
the broom; no, the scythe was whispering to
itself, hidden in the long grass

where the mower let it drop, distracted
by something sweeter than fact or fire.

"Perfect Weather for Hanging Wash"

The church bell rings one time.
It could be one o'clock
or half past any hour.
How quickly I can do nothing.

At dinner we fill each other's
glasses with wine and spoon the soup
into each bowl. Someone makes a fire,
someone slices bread. We all talk.

Walking down to the beach today—
the blue Mediterranean
behind the white houses, I thought
of my mother—what she would say.

My Mother's Secret Life

At the table or leaning on the counter,
sometimes—if there was a lull or a little
space between the afternoon and starting
supper, we could get my mother to draw

horses, and every horse was perfect:
fine head and arched neck, the ears pitched forward
inquisitively, shoulders and back sloped
and shadowed with a curve, and then the legs—

long and shapely, tapered to the ankle
and hooves: running, galloping, standing still,
a horse we would want to keep, a prototype
of all the ones we'd meet in books, later.

As for the guitar up in the attic,
we never asked what she could do with that.

The Exam

It is mid-October. The trees are in
their autumnal glory (red, yellow-green,

orange) outside the classroom where students
take the midterm, sniffling softly as if

identifying lines from Blake or Keats
was such sweet sorrow, summoned up in words

they never saw before. I am thinking
of my parents, of the six decades they've

been together, of the thirty thousand
meals they've eaten in the kitchen, of the

more than twenty thousand nights they've slept
under the same roof. I am wondering

who could have fashioned the test that would have
predicted this success? Who could have known?

Grandma Clara

About noon she arrived in her blue-and-
white Bel Air by Chevrolet, in which she
did not see the USA but only

the road from her house in town to the farm
she built with her husband, who died as soon
as they retired, and that is why she came

each day—just to have something to do, to
help us with the work we had inherited
from her: the strawberry fields, gardens,

apple orchards, and grapevines, rhubarb stalks,
potato patch, rows of sweet corn, wild plums,
and gooseberries—and all those fields of corn

and oats and hay, pastures too, above the
house and woods or down by the meadow where
the green grass grew. Who would not return to

such a place? I see her walking across
the lawn in her straw hat, hoe in hand,
ready to chop away whatever weeds

dared grow between the perfectly mounded
hills of potatoes, those rows that would feed
us all through the cold white winter when she

would come less often though we would see her
every morning in the back of church—
praying, no doubt, for the whole crop of us.

September Afternoon, Writing

In my grandmother's time,
the afternoon was filled
with apples—apple peelings, apple
cores, apple pies, and applesauce.

In the afternoons, there were
grapes turning purple on the vines
at the garden's edge, pumpkins
ripening in the last warm days.

I came walking home from school,
carrying an empty lunch box
and a bag of homework.
I can't remember any of that.

My grandmother would have
wondered what I am doing here—
without a decent paring knife,
and these pages filled with scribbling.

My Grandmother Sells Her Strawberry Field

That would have been the year my brother Rick
was born, the year my brother Kevin turned

one; my sister Nancy was about three;
my brother Dan was four (or five—it all

depends on when it happened). I was
eleven; my sister Betty was nine

(or ten), and my brothers Mike and Joe were
eight and seven (close enough). We were all

so young! My parents were thirty-something,
and though my grandmother was sixty-three,

she'd been a widow for almost ten years.
That would have been the year she decided

that a strawberry field doesn't have to
last forever, and love is all there is.

The Queen of Summer Lawns

Someone must be queen of the afternoon.
Someone must sit at the top of the steps
with a dark pink hollyhock in her hair.

We must call her "Your Majesty"
and scatter roses and petunia
petals on the steps before her. She must

wear a dandelion bracelet and a
crown of grape leaves. She must sit very still.
When she is thirsty, we will give her red

nectar to drink; when she is hungry, we
will feed her vegetables from the garden.
We will guard her kingdom from the gravel

road to the apple trees. No stranger shall
approach her: winter winds will stay away
forever, and the snows will never come.

My Sister's School Papers

Her handwriting is very different from mine.
I'm messier. I write larger and spell better
because I haven't been lying in bed for months,
lost in the heart's faltering chambers.

Most of the papers are arithmetic problems
and worksheets about stories they've read.
For example: "In the story, 'The Boy
with the Bass Drum,' Joey prays because
(a) the parade was a success, (b) he discovered
the horrors of war, (c) he wanted his father to return
safely, or (d) he was grateful not to be hungry."
"d"—My sister got that one right, and I can tell
she had read the story because if she hadn't,
she would have guessed "b" ("he discovered
the horrors of war").

It's a long worksheet in six parts,
and she misses only one question on the first page.
The "Vocabulary Section" and "Recalling Details"
are perfect, and she sorts the adverbs
from the verbs and the compound words (no problem),
but in the section that requires her to divide
each word into syllables and place the primary accent,
she gets every one of them wrong—
she loses seventeen points on fifteen words!
I realize she must have been missing the day
they learned about stress, too tired and pale
even to be carried up the steps to the classroom.

Later, I'll call my brother and tell him
that in the quiz about Paraguay, she got every
question right, including the capital (Asunción)
and the name of the native people (the Guaraní),
but—no surprise—she misspelled Jesuit.

Generally, she does well in religion tests, but
her essays are very cautious. I know this because
I am in one and am much better behaved than I
ever was in real life. I like the way she ends
her essay about "What a Catholic Education
Means to Me": "When I am older," she says,
"my education will help me understand more things
in the world and help me get to heaven."
I hope at least one of those things is true.

Two Girls on a Hayrack

We're elbow to elbow,
hip to hip, my right arm to her
left, her left knee to my right.

Our feet are dangling down.
Someone has put us there
on the wagon, someone who

is holding the camera—a Brownie
Instamatic—who has stepped back
in order to get the entire rack

and its beautiful shadow
into the picture. It's afternoon
says the way the light falls;

it's hot says the ground.
"We're alive," say the girls.
"Click" goes the camera.

The Blue in the Distance

The blue in the distance is April,
and April is coming up the meadow,
crossing the river at the place where
the rocks line up like beads on a
string, and we can walk across in
August—but not in April when the
waters are deep and move swiftly
under the slow skin warming in the sun.

The gold light falling into the blue
is the past, that other country where
the fields are undivided and houses
came with barns and silos and sheds
or go to live with other houses in
a place called town. That is how
the past was in the golden light.
Now there are houses everywhere.

The line on the horizon is very
thin and black. It draws the twig
on the branch and the branch on
the tree. It divides the ground
from the sky and follows the hill
up and down the valley—
whatever comes, whatever goes,
that line will carry it to your eye.

The green is the most surprising
thing of all. It comes up from
the ground, comes through
the branches in the air, comes
after the black, blue, and the gold.
The green grass, the green leaf,
the green dress that we wear
all summer long and into the grave.

Things I Know

I know how the cow's head turns
to gaze at the child in the hay aisle;

I know the way the straw shines
under the one bare light in the barn.

How a chicken pecks gravel into silt
and how the warm egg rests beneath

the feathers—I know that too, and
what to say, watching the rain slide

in silver chains over the machine
shed's roof. I know how one pail

of water calls to another and how
it sloshes and spills when I walk

from the milk house to the barn.
I know how the barn fills and

then empties, how I scatter lime
on the walk, how I sweep it up.

In the silo, I know the rung under
my foot; on the tractor, I know

the clutch and the throttle; I slip
through the fence and into the woods,

where I know everything: trunk
by branch by leaf into sky.

Bell Bottom Baby

When she was one I cut
a pattern in blue denim

and sewed the pieces together.
Simplicity simple, elastic waistband.

The pants flared out into bells
with one-inch cuffs at the bottom,

but the part that amazes me is how
I sat for hours with an embroidery hoop,

stitching a Jacobean flower garden
to trail down each small leg,

knowing how quickly she'd
grow out of everything I did.

The Suzuki Mother

That was me, standing
behind the child,
adjusting the violin
on her shoulder,
straightening the wrist
so that it formed a perfect
angle, elbow to hand,
fingers placed squarely upon
the yellow lines
that crossed the fret board.

That was me, humming along
as I watched the music,
counting silently, hoping
each note into being,
more disciplined for them
than I'd ever been for myself
when I practiced piano in the sunporch,
skipping the hardest notes,
ignoring the fingerings—
all drama and flourish.

And that was me too,
thinking I had no expectations,
that I only wanted them
to find something they loved
and do it well—
when the truth was I wanted
an Itzhak Perlman
or a Yehudi Menuhin—
a little prodigy to call my own.

We Have Come This Far

After you died, everything changed.
When I could no longer talk to you
I told myself things you said years
before. I thought of you as many
different people at once, old and young.

After you died, you could see into
the future and explain the past. Often
I would sit out in my chair on the lawn
and listen to you all afternoon. I asked
for advice, and yours was always good.

Of course it took some time before we
reached this happiness. I am aware
that you may have gone on to do other
things, that this world may no longer
concern you, but for me this is a way

to remember you. I suppose I don't
need to say that you are well now,
cured of that thing that killed you,
and planning to buy outrageous
hats and travel more frequently.

You're the only one I listen to
some days. Your sense of humor has
returned, and often we laugh all night.
As you may have noticed, I have been
adding color to everything, because

I know that pleases you. I hear you
telling me to love the things of this world—
the white pines, the sumac, flowers
in gardens, and shells on the shore.
I see them with your eyes and say I do.

Next Time

I'll know the names of all of the birds
and flowers, and not only that, I'll
tell you the name of the piano player
I'm hearing right now on the kitchen
radio, but I won't be in the kitchen,

I'll be walking a street in
New York or London, about
to enter a coffee shop where people
are reading or working on their
laptops. They'll look up and smile.

Next time I won't waste my heart
on anger; I won't care about
being right. I'll be willing to be
wrong about everything and to
concentrate on giving myself away.

Next time, I'll rush up to people I love,
look into their eyes, and kiss them, quick.
I'll give everyone a poem I didn't write,
one specially chosen for that person.
They'll hold them up and see a new
world. We'll sing the morning in,

and I will keep in touch with friends,
writing long letters when I wake from
a dream where they appear on the
Orient Express. "Meet me in Istanbul,"
I'll say, and they will.

Dominoes

It's partly about dumb luck
and partly about getting rid of
things that will count against you
when someone goes out. Someone

goes out because they are lucky,
because they pay attention, and
because they put down the right
thing at just the right time

and you don't. You know
that you will always lose this game,
but you play it anyway because
you love the little boneyard in

the middle of the table and how,
for a few moments after each game,
you see your own hands shuffling
the bones along with the familiar

hands of your mother and your father
who are telling stories that make you
forget to put down the double blank,
or to look over to see that someone

who has been lucky and paying attention
is just about to go out . . . but honestly
who cares? Someone has to lose,
and why shouldn't that someone be you?

The Last Perfect Season

No one knew it then, but that was the last
perfect season, the last time sky and earth

were so balanced that when we walked,
we flew, the last time we could pick a crate

of strawberries every morning in June,
the last time the mystical threshing

machine appeared at the edge of the field,
dividing the oats from the chaff, time of

hollyhocks and sprinklers, white clouds over
a tin roof. Everyone we knew was young then.

Our mothers wore dresses the color of
dove wings, slim at the waist, skirts flaring

just enough to let the folds drape slightly,
like the elegant suits our fathers wore,

shirts so white they dazzled even
the grainy eye of the camera when

we looked down into the viewfinder to
press the button that would keep us there,

as if we already knew that this was
as good as it was ever going to get.

SELECTIONS FROM
MODERN LOVE & OTHER MYTHS

Whiteout

I have been, all morning, inside a book.
When I look up it is snowing—heavy
snow—and the wind is making a steady
run across the ridge of my neighbor's roof.

Everything is white-blurred, taken down
a shade, softened and yet forbidding, as
if warning that walking into snow is
different and more dangerous, as if

winter and cold had a hold on us
that summer never did. How quickly our
footprints disappear on a day like this,
and, after an hour or two, even a

body could be lost for months. I turn back
to the page where there was a fire burning.

On the Shortest Days

At almost four in the afternoon, the
wind picks up and sifts through the golden woods.

The bare tree trunks bronze and redden, branches
on fire in the heavy sky that flickers

with the disappearing sun. I wonder
what I owe the fading day, why I keep

my place at this dark desk by the window
measuring the force of the wind, gauging

how long a certain cloud will hold that pink
edge that even now has slipped into gray?

Quickly the lights are appearing, a lamp
in every window and nests of stars

on the rooftops. Ladders lean against the hills
and people climb, rung by rung, into the night.

Winter's Night

We are standing at the door after a party,
and a man I don't know very well says that

I should write a poem about the moon
and the winter's night, and now I wonder

what he had in mind—something about
a black branch against the white snow?

Or something about the way we all hesitated
to leave that house filled with wine and

flowers to linger in the cold—the cold,
which might be what he wanted me

to write about—the cold that cracks the house
at midnight and slices through the air

like a sword slipping into its sheath,
or the sound of ice-skaters on the lake,

their blades cutting slivers of the moon
into the dark surface of the winter's night.

Like That

I could not remember the beginning
line, which is almost as if to say I

could not remember my name—but that (too)
has happened, and I've survived. Memory

is like a sieve, a fringe made of fingers
trying to hold to the hem of the ocean—

the tide comes in, the tide goes out—green lung.
The thing I forgot was that we grow old

and find those "deep trenches" in "beauty's field,"
and I forgot because something else kept

coming to mind—a line about "nodding
by the fire," someone loving my "pilgrim soul."

Though everything else may slip away,
I won't forget I once was loved like that.

It's Amazing

Another word for that is astonishing
or astounding, remarkable, or marvelous.

It's also slightly startling, which leads to
shocking and upsetting, perhaps a bit

disquieting, and that is troubling and
distressing—you could say outrageous

and deplorable, which leads to wicked
and more precise equations such as

sinful and immoral or just plain bad
and wrong. It's amazing, which is just to say

bewildering and unexpected, that
it happened out of the blue, and that we went

all the way from miraculous to absurd,
within the syllables of just one word.

The Hampstead Sonnets
(The Real Thing)

That was the day I knew, although even
earlier—in Bristol, after we'd been
to Cornwall and back again—I could tell
something was happening to us, something
I wasn't expecting, something unplanned,
uncharted, and entirely amazing.
(I've looked up that word, "amazing," and put
it in another poem that explains
what happened much better than this will.) You
came down to London from the North because
I'd invited you, and even though I
never thought you'd come, you came, and I was
waiting when you rang the bell, and I was there
on Hampstead Heath watching the sun go down,
and then we went inside and fell in love.

We went inside and fell in love—easy
as I am telling it. Our shoulders touched
or didn't touch—it doesn't matter now—
but I could hardly breathe; I think I swooned
(when I'd never believed it possible);
I think my face went pale; I think my heart
was beating wildly—yes, I'm sure it was.
Next day we went to Richmond and to Kew
and walked through the palm house and the gardens,
admiring the gryphons and other beasts,
finding the pagoda disappointing,
the cactus houses overdone, but the
rhododendron grove was perfect: look at
the two of us, surrounded by flowers.

Later, the picture of the two of us
surrounded by all those flowers would go

into the fire with the other pictures
he found. Later, the letters that you wrote
would escape the fire and go for years
unread. Later—but what's the point? Later
is now, and now is too late to wonder what
we might have done with that amazing love
that came to us when we least expected
it, when we didn't know how rare it was,
when we—but I really most blame myself—
were afraid of saying the truth, afraid
the whole world would come down on its pillars,
afraid to hurt anyone else but us.

Anyone else but us might have made it
work; anyone else but me might have said
"Yes, wait," anyone else but you might have
asked again, but because of the distance,
because of the differences, because
of the dangers, the darkness, the dread nights
of the soul, I let all these things swallow
our words and then, for many years, silence
was all there was between us. Your letters
(and you'll never know how fiercely I fought
to keep them) went first to a friend's closet
and then, when I made the break I couldn't
make earlier, to my own apartment,
and then to my house where I live alone.

I live alone by choice and for pleasure,
and you have the life I had when we met.
I was a wife then; now you're a husband
and the father of daughters, just as you
hoped. Sometimes I remember us walking

on the beach in Cornwall, gathering slate,
"for pure and useless beauty" as you said,
and how we went later for tea and scones
and how later we slept on the cliff's edge
and (years later) I met you on a bridge
over the Thames just as I was thinking
of how once we had walked there together,
just as I wondered if that amazing
love we had was truly (yes) the real thing.

Bird on a Wall in County Clare

Looks like a piebald rook,
a pinto crow. Portly, black-
stockinged, bright-eyed.

Walks along the flat slate
top-of-the-wall, head moving back
and forth on the rocker of his neck.

Stops, walks again, walks until
he reaches the last slate. Pauses,
glancing this way and then that.

Stands, steadies himself like a child
on the high dive. Gathers up his
strength and throws himself into the air.

The Last Straw

Some days you can lose just about
anything. Things can break in your
hands, rip loose in the wind, fall from
the shelf. They can go down the
drain, slip through a crack, roll off the

edge. And you? You just shrug your
shoulders, smile a wry little smile,
and say, "Ah, c'est-ce la vie," or maybe,
"So it goes," and "That's the way the
cookie crumbles, baby." Other days,

spilling coffee on the counter makes
you weep; you see the toast crumbs
on the floor and curse your carelessness.
The whole world seems in pieces
because of leaves fallen from the

hibiscus plant, and when you see
that its red blossoms opened (at last!)
when you were gone and dropped like
ashes to the carpet—it's the
last straw; it just breaks your heart.

Things to Watch While You Drive

The trees, slipping
across the fields, changing places with
barns and silos,

the hills, rolling over
on command, their bellies
green and leafy,

the sun-tiger, riding
on your rooftop, its shadow racing
up and down the ditches,

a flock of birds,
carrying the sky by the corners,
a giant sheet of blue,

the road, always
twisting toward or away from you—
both, at the same time.

The Idea of Living

It has its attractions,
chiefly visual: all those

shapes and lines, hunks
of color and light (the way

the gold light falls across
the lawn in early summer,

the iridescent blue floating
on the lake at sunset),

and being alive seems
to be a necessity if you want

to sit in the sun or rub your
toes in the sand at the beach.

You need to be breathing
in order to eat paella and

drink sangria, and making love
is quite impossible without

a body, unless you are one
of those, given—like gold—
to spin in airy thinness forever.

The Lost Prophecy

What did you say about the moon?
Was it good? Was the moon a good
sign? Should we trust how it silvers
the hills and follow after it?

And what will happen to the fields
and the woods? Who will love
them when we are gone? And when
will that be? How long do we have?

And justice? Will there be justice?
How will it come, and will it be
mixed with mercy? Where will such
wisdom be found in all the earth?

Who will be watching then, who
listening? How will the things that are
coming be noticed by those who never
look up? The moon will be there.

What did you say about the moon?

One Thousand and One Nights

*

After the first night,
it was easy. He had a taste
for plot, and it turned out
that I was good at suspension
like the man who walked
a tightrope
between the towers—

I touched down
and never flew again,
but that's another one
of those stories.
Swans came into it
of course—the bell beat
of their wings and things
like that. My brother's hat,
my father in the city,
my mother scrubbing
floors, and my
sister (finally, my
sister) and then . . .

*

I was sitting at my desk
when I heard a woman's cry,
but when I looked, I
saw that there was no one
there, and I realized
the cry must have come
from another time
and it was my own voice
I heard as I had heard it

speaking in another language
saying all the mysteries
at once, melting into
the most liquid of tongues.
I bent my head to read.
I cut the fabric into pieces
and put it back
together, differently.

*

Patterns,
it seems, are a way
of losing one's way
and also of coming home
again, but you can't
(I can't, we can't) go home
again—we've known that
from the beginning,
and so it would be a surprise
to find it (that is, home) has
been waiting for us all along.
The pages in his book
are empty. Another deception.
Somewhere it is all written
down in long scrolls—
or somewhere all the words are
burning, dissolving into
the wordless song of birds.

The Poem You Said You Wouldn't Write

The poem you said you wouldn't write
is the one that I find myself reading this

morning, and even though I should be doing
something else, I find I can't help writing

this poem about the sunlit patterns falling across
my desk, the sounds of cars starting up

in the neighborhood, and how it helps
to have these poems from you, the evidence

of things unseen, the substance of hope
that there will always be someone—the boy

sitting out on the front step with his transistor
radio, listening to news about Fidel Castro, or

the man sitting in his green lawn chair
watching how sky can be emptied of leaf,

branch, and trunk, until nothing is left
but stump and sawdust and your poem

about the tree, the one you said you wouldn't
write, the one that holds the branches high.

The One Constant Thing

We were talking about death
over the phone, speaking words into
a mouthpiece, listening to them
coming back into our ears.

I was looking out across the backyard,
taking in the curve of a tree
and the tall grasses dead in the swamp.
The light was early and golden.

You did not tell me, but I knew
that you could see—across the city
from sixty stories up—the lakes
and streets stretched out for miles.

I agree that whatever it is, it won't be
like this. I want to say I share your sense that
there will be someone there to meet us.
Yes, I suppose it's all we think about.

Death, Inc.

Without his scythe and crooked knife
he's simply an ordinary guy.

You see him at the bus stop,
and he's reading a folded newspaper,

or he's in the car next to you
on the freeway—first he passes

you, and then you pass him.
It goes on like that for a long time,

but though you glance over at him,
he never looks back at you,

which (it turns out) is a good thing.
All the while you've been

waiting for the carriage to stop
(kindly) at your door—the carriage

that would take you past the schoolyard
and the fields, accompanied by

the gentle clip-clop of horses' hooves,
but suddenly you realize he might be

driving an eighteen-wheeler, high on
meth, tires screeching. Yes—it could

happen like that, but it's just
as likely he might be the shadow

of a tree you planted years ago
falling across the green lawn.

Even in My Time

Even in my time kingdoms fell,
and islands disappeared beneath the waves,
borders opened, and walls came down.
There were so many countries I would never see.

And even in my time, one tree died
and another one grew tall. The sky opened
and then closed, very slowly. Letters turned
yellow, and curtains faded in the window.

Friends who were once so dark and handsome
grew old. Bones in their spines crumbled,
or tumors filled the soft place under their
ribs. Sometimes their hearts stopped beating.

Even in my time, there were gardens filled
with flowers that would only last the day.

The Posthumous Journey of the Soul

What to bring along? Nothing.
Everything. Even the smallest rock
is too heavy to lift, and whether
you can carry even a bird's song
in your ear is uncertain.

And where to go? Not back along
those roads you knew when you
were living in the body—not even
into the dreams that came at night—
but somewhere out there, beyond
anything you have imagined.

There are some things you will recognize:
a palm tree beyond the last thought,
a thing with feathers that perches in the soul,
and a woman, lovely in her bones.
Once you pass the gate, it will be only
you . . . and the windy sky.

All the People I Used to Be

I was the kind of woman who brought
fresh bread and butter to class;
I tilted my head to hear your childhood—
just the sound of it as the trains passed
and the waves rolled onto the shore.

It was my intention to be with you
as long as you needed me, but you never
did (need me). I was the kind of woman
people don't mention, I was very ordinary—
except for that heart of mine when it loved.

I used to be able to keep still—one
hand held the needle as the thread passed through;
I filled the cup to the brim and carried
it across the room, and when I wrote that
last word, you could see each letter clearly.

For the Evening Light

If you listen carefully, you'll hear
at least five kinds of birdsong
threaded through the air.
It isn't necessary to name them.

That sound a minute ago was a train whistle.
Even though it is very quiet now
you must not forget that somewhere
a train is moving through the woods.

Practice this way of letting go:
put your fingers around a rose
and twist it off the stem. Scatter
the petals to the wind.

Tell yourself the truth about him
and then erase it. Go to the window
where the light has disappeared
behind the trees. Say goodbye.

Say It

Say that it is the continuous life
you desire, that one day might stretch into
the next without a seam, without seeming
to move one minute away from the past
or that in passing through whatever comes

you keep coming to the faces you love,
never leaving them entirely behind.

Say that it is simply a wish to waste
time forever, lingering with the friends
you've gathered together, a gradual
illumination traveling the spine,
eyes brimming with the moment that is now.

Say that it is the impulse of the soul
to endure forever. Say it again.

The Book of Hours

There was that one hour sometime
in the middle of the last century.
It was autumn, and I was in my father's
woods, building a house out of branches
and the leaves that were falling like
thousands of letters from the sky.

And there was that one in Central Park
in the middle of the seventies.
We were sitting on a blanket, listening
to Pete Seeger singing "This land is
your land, this land is my land," and
the Vietnam War was finally over.

I would definitely include an hour
spent in one of the galleries of the
Tate Britain, looking up at the
painting of *King Cophetua and
the Beggar Maid*, and, afterward
the walk along the Thames, and

I would also include one of those
hours when I woke in the night and
couldn't get back to sleep thinking
about how nothing I thought was going
to happen happened the way I expected,
and things I never expected to happen did,

just like that hour today, when we saw
the dog running along the busy road
and we stopped and held on to her
until her owner came along and brought
her home—that was an hour well
spent. Yes, that was a keeper.

SELECTIONS FROM *THE GREEN HOUSE*

Irish Suite

On the way to the airport, we argue
about whether or not I should call you
when I have arrived on the other side
of the world the next day in the middle
of your night. You say, "That's what lovers do.
They call to let each other know when they're
safely there wherever it is they've gone,
and when they come back they call to say they're
on their way." "I didn't know there were rules
like that," I say. "Who made you King of Hearts?"

On the airplane, I eat the pretend food
they pretend to give me, munching fat-free
pretzels and pouring things from aluminum
into plastic. A lime wedge (slightly brown
at the edges) floats among the ice cubes.
Through the clouds, a road—no, a river!—
appears and then slips under the broad
wing just behind the lozenge of window.
After that the clouds—ice-cream castles in
the air—are blocking out the earth below.

When I am there, the wind pushes the clouds
over the high ridge. A horse, galloping,
is the one moving piece of horizon.
On the road below the window, two cars,
a blue Mercedes and a silver one,
file by (like dogs on a scent). I count shades
of green and listen to the wind pounding
against the glass. Out there, the horse is a
rock, rocking at the gate; the sea seeps through
the clouds and spreads silver across the bay.

What does it mean that I am writing this
and staying in the same house the famous
poet stayed in (or, if not this one, then
one just like it, with its identical
wild-eyed cow and tufts of grass, the actual
blue inlet there, beyond the limestone hills)?
Did Emily Dickinson's fly buzz then
as it does now, flying madly around
the room while I watch the Irish cows graze
and the four horses coming through the gate?

Nothing neat, nothing too pretty about
this place; everything in casual
disarray: slates leaned up against the wall,
gold flowers between the stones in the driveway.
Even the cows across the road arrange
themselves randomly on the field as if
tossed like dice from a giant's hand.
Down to the sea, the clouds scuttle the hills,
tipping up to one side, a streak of blue
unexpectedly coming through, then sun.

On the road to Cork (and on the way back
again), we counted up years in children
and marriages. Without meaning to
I spilled a bitter story, and you told
me a thing or two in return. The car
sped through the green fields, up and down the hills
and though our hearts went open and wild, we
(neither of us) showed it on our faces.
On the road to Cork (and on the way back
again) we measured our voices in years.

That morning, walking on the beach between
Liscannor and Lahinch, we stepped from rock
to reach the sand and then crossed pools
until we reached the smooth stretch of gold
and gray and black shore, sifted and swirled
together, rippled into waterless
waves that carried us east until we missed
one of the dogs and called to her despite
the wind that pushed our cries behind us as
we looked toward the graveyard of the land.

I made myself walk along the open
cliff, sick to my stomach at the closeness
of the edge, watching the opposite cliff, I
saw a man dangle over the side and turned
away, waiting for the crowd to moan when
he fell (as I felt he would), but the wind
kept up its gentle push, and the people
streamed by with their cameras. A phone rang
and someone answered it: "Cliffs of Moher—
could you hold please? Hang on, I'll find him now."

The open sky is my comfort; over
and above me I fall into it and
let it fall into me. I ask the sky
what it is I should be forgiven for
and then I bow my head to the gravel road
pulled by thistle and vetch, stepping aside
to let the lone car pass, regaining the
way, whistling a little old-timey song.
It's the open sky I love, the way it
lifts up over the hills and cliffs like wings.

A Bird in County Clare

This morning's minion was white shouldered,
sat on the stone wall, not caught by the wind.
Slow and heavy, awkward on his thin bird
legs, he hopped sideways down the wall and stopped.

There would be no bright buckling here, no flash
of crimson gold, as the cloud and land split
open. I watched his huddled shape, feathers
blowing like the grasses in a ditch, stay

Earthbound, head bowed, his dull eye turned
away from the house, his wings tucked roughly
behind his back as he noticed the complete
absence of branch and leaf, which I now saw

For the first time when I wondered what song
he might have sung, in what bare ruined choir.

A Postcard from the Burren

The quarry down the hill is deep,
its walls no different
than those of the ruined houses

we pass when we go to find
the horses: doorways gaped open,
dirt floors, the view going through

to the hillside where bushes
still yield berries, sweet
purples in the long green grass.

We do not know who lived there.
The sound of them is long gone,
echoing past Jupiter,

but the stones they stood
still stand as if to wish us here.

At Clonmacnoise

As soon as we stopped the car
he was there—first
on the branch,
then the wall, and then
coming up to
the opened door, happy
to see us—it seemed—
at Clonmacnoise.

We were thinking of ships in the air,
but instead we saw
this red-breasted ruin-lover,
guardian of the marvelous, flying
against the wind
though the open arches
and roofless sanctuary
to where a monk
once knelt, praising God

for the dreams that made
him sing his songs,
turning them over
in the sweetness
of hay in the crib and milk
in the wooden bucket,
exactly the way this bird
made his given call.

Playing the Pipes

This morning in Dingle, the clouds
bellied down over the mountains
and broke into gray, white, and blue.

Winds flagged through the palm trees
that the man from the "Big House"
brought back to the bay long ago.

Up Greene Street, the schoolkids
in their dark uniforms gather
on the sidewalk by the Spar store.

Long ago, this was a Spanish town,
east of the Blasket Island and west of
Connor Pass. The harbor is full of sails.

The piper sits in his little shop
on the rounding road, selling penny-
whistles, telling anyone who will listen

how many ways there are
to vary the sound, how much
there is to think of all at once.

This Beautiful Paper

Tonight, in an old notebook
on the reverse side of a scribbled

poem that never got off
the ground (a poem that kept

going back to the starting line
and flapping its paper wings),

I decided to be thankful for the pen
in a hand that can still hold it,

still make the ink into letters,
the letters into words that are

worlds no matter how tiny and
almost indecipherable. Tonight

I love the faint blue horizons
that cross the page, waiting

to be filled with golden light
as if in a Rembrandt painting.

Snow, Snow, Snow

All the good words are gone now.
Silly to think I might say something new,

something you couldn't have said better,
letters rearranged or changed

from first thought (best)
to second (not better). I imagine

the snow-filled fields, crisscrossed
by roads and animal tracks,

and you at your desk, then
asleep on the couch,

the fire burning low
in the cast-iron stove.

How amazing that we share
this page with its deep and obscure

drifts—how right that we
might make a meeting out of snow

and resume our quiet walk through
the deep and lonely nights.

The Sound of a Train

Everyone imagines the poem
they would write if they were you.

They think that almost anything
that happens is good material

and that you are always waiting
for the hidden poem to appear.

They want to see you take a
coin from behind someone's ear,

they want to know the words
to the song in the distance.

The poem they imagine is better
than anything you will ever write.

The poem they imagine is so good
that you have stopped trying to write it.

Writing Poetry

First I ask them to fly.
We start by standing
on top of the desk
in the classroom, but later
we open the windows and
circle the campus, our
fingers touching the bright
tip of the chapel spire.

Next we do transformations:
water into wine, stones into
bread—the usual. Once
they've got the hang of it,
some of them like to spend
the day as various kinds of
animals and trees. At night
the astronomy class
notices constellations
that appear to be just
overhead, accompanied
by electric guitars.

The most difficult thing
we do is to sit in our chairs
very quietly and dive
deep into the ocean
in search of a pearl
(you know the one).
For now, we're building
up our lungs, seeing how
long we can stay under.

Why We Need Poetry

How would I know that I loved the Lions
on the steps of the Public Library

if Elizabeth Bishop hadn't called them
"agreeable" and promised they would rise

and pace through the open door up into
the reading rooms? And who would tell me

how to ride along with Death—except,
of course, Emily, who also told me

about Hope, that sturdy little thing with
feathers, singing its heart out in the storm.

When the Colonel swept the ears to the floor
and they were pressed there, listening, who would

have told their story, if not for poetry?
And how could it be the world we turn to

without knowing, unless it is our only
way to say what we feel about living

in the body? How can I learn to stand
and wait without it? Who will compare me

to a summer's day? If not for poetry,
I would not know that small birds sigh, that

butterflies sleep, that fish smile, and that words
are riprap, making a place for us to walk.

Reading the Notes in the *Norton Anthology of Poetry*

Some people need to be told that pullets
are chickens and that Nicollet Island

and the Guthrie are Minneapolis
landmarks. Other people (or maybe the

same ones) don't know that New Jersey is
across the Hudson from New York City's

West Side and that Stonehenge is a circle
of great standing stones on Salisbury Plain.

Some people might need to be reminded
that the Civil War ended in Eighteen-

sixty-five, and that Homer was reported
to be blind. Personally, I didn't know

that Isadora Duncan was strangled
when her scarf caught in the wheel of her car,

and I wouldn't know that a ball turret
gunner had to be a short man, though I

knew, because he "hunched in its belly" that
he looked like a fetus in a womb. And

I knew all of the words to the song in
Lowell's "Skunk Hour" and that love was "careless."

I knew too that John Keats loved Fanny Brawne,
though I'm not so sure he'd have loved kumquats.

I wish, that in addition to the things
that make up a mint julep, the editors

had given the proportions; I wish that
I could scratch the word "peat" and smell the fire

in some small cottage under Ben Bulben.
Someday I hope to hear a corncrake's cry.

The Birds Walking

I love to watch the birds walking.
Some are so contemplative:
they tuck their wings behind their backs
and gaze into the tangled earth.

Others walk in pairs, bowing to each other
as they talk about who's in and who's out.
"All the world's a cage," one says.
"I am not the golden bird" says the other.

Then a bird falls from the sky, and they disperse,
pecking at the uneven tips of green grass.
The shadows of wings ripple through the light
and over the bent backs of the birds on the ground.

I love to watch the birds walking,
to see them climb the staircase of the sky.

The Cardinal

The cardinal who crashed
into my window
is lying on the patio
like a blossom fallen from
an amaryllis in January.

His tiny feet are pointed
to the sky; he is so lately dead
it seems that he could fly,
except that his eyes are shut
above his mask; his wings

are neatly tucked, and his
head rests on its broken stem.
He is so lovely lying there
I do not want to move him,
but later, before the coyotes

come, I will carry him to
the marsh and fling him out—
along with branches from
the storm, a raku cup, and
a gold ring I'll never wear again.

Still Life

On the desk, brocaded cloth and
a brass lamp. Numbers in columns and
a scattering of pens. Keys on a ring.

Remember the way time used to fly
with calendar wings? The years
went by like shuffled cards, a flip

book that made the cat play a jig
on his fiddle and the cow jump over
the moon. How mysterious.

I do not think I am afraid to die.
I think that dying does not frighten me.
I am not thinking about being dead.

Just when I thought the poem was
over I heard a train in the distance,
and now a car is climbing the road.

Constable Clouds

How is it that the sky looks more
like a painting than the painting

looks like the sky? How does that
maple do color—as if a brush

dipped in orange had swept over
it as it passed, leaving just

that blush of orange on the green?
How is air thinner than the distance

between things? How is depth
deeper when you look away

and back again? How is it possible
that this moment (leaves falling

from the maples, blackbirds)
is shorter than eternity?

Bird Song, Cannon River Bottoms

I stopped for the sound,
thinking of the end of Keats's ode,
"To Autumn."

The cars on the distant road
replaced the lamb's loud bleat,
and bicyclists went whirling by.

Then choruses
of trills and twitterings
filled the stadium of the air—

then faded away
as quickly as they came.
Two men on Rollerblades went by,

a siren wailed.
I heard the sound of wings
. . . and slowly it started up again—

a tweet, a chirp,
a long sentence in a language
that may have been lark.

Good

I'm good at being where
I should be when I shouldn't be,

at saying the almost right
thing at exactly the wrong

time. I'm good at indecision,
good at leaving just as the

blizzard is about to begin,
finally selling that piece

of land as the market crashes.
I'm good at spiderwebs and

finding tiny agates; if you
lost something I'm good at

finding it where you've already
looked twenty times before.

I'm good at forgetting,
forgiving everything that

happened, happy just to sit
with you watching clouds—

I've always been good at
watching clouds and listening

to you talk, so just keep talking
and I'll listen. I'm good at that.

The Cup

Yesterday, in the café,
how beautiful the cup

that held your tea—
the yellow tea in the

clear glass, and the flowers
in the shimmering pouch,

and how well you told
the stories that fit

into the hour (which
lasted exactly as long

as a cup of tea) in the
clear blue tint of the glass

and how . . . "comfortable"
(I thought) I've always

felt with you. Even in
the rain, which you

promised would come,
I'm remembering

the cup—how beautiful
the cup—in the yellow café.

NEW POEMS

I. Luck

Those Hours

There were moments, hours even,
when it was clear what I

was meant to do, as if
a landscape had revealed itself

in the morning light.
I could see the road

plainly now, imagining myself
walking towards the distant mountains

like a pilgrim in the old stories—
ready to take on any danger,

hapless but always hopeful,
certain that my simple belief

in the light
would be enough.

Someone Just Like You

(for all those who crossed the Mississippi River on the I-35w
Bridge before it fell at 6:05 p.m., CDT, on August 1, 2007)

Whoever you were—crossing the bridge
earlier in the day—you went from one side
to the other, barely noticing the river,
the way you were held up in the sky
by a fragile and faulty design.

You crossed over, one car in a lane
of blue, silver, and black, tapping your
fingers on the wheel, changing the station
to catch the weather report, picking up your
cell phone to say you were on the way home.

You were early that day—or a bit later,
but everything else was about the same,
though the bridge shook slightly, a bird
flew out from beneath the railing,
someone looked up and saw a flash of blue.

It only took a minute and you were
headed north or south, and someone
else was crossing—someone just like you,
feeling the sky falling, the world collapsing
beneath them, that other side now
more impossible than the moon.

In Iowa City One Night

I swear there is only one cicada
in Minnesota—no choruses in the trees
as there were in Iowa City
the time we drove in from the East,
racing the golden light down the interstate
to arrive at evening and walk the streets
near Prairie Lights Books.

It was a Sunday, and the lights
in the store were out,
but we could see the names
of the latest and greatest poets of America
in the window display—
their books posed like beautiful
paper mannequins.

Later, we found a place to eat
down and around the corner
from the Deadwood, where you
used to come looking for your son,
and I know you were afraid back then
and did the only thing you could think of,
because waiting is not your style,

and because you will always find the lost ones,
those who have missed the last bus home,
those who might be grateful for the ride
that comes along when all hope has gone,
for the shadow
coming out of the night
that turns out to be you.

Primitive

How lucky we are that we do not live
in the time of the Plague, when, in three

years a third of Europe's population—
20 million people—died, and no one

knew the cause. How fortunate we
are to know that it was not the planets

or the wrath of God that caused it
but a tiny bacillus carried by fleas

on the backs of rats coming by ship
from Asia, and how much better it is

to live now, rather than in 1891, when
Thomas Edison filed patents for

the first motion picture camera and viewer,
which operated on a perceptual phenomenon

called "persistence of vision"—a thing that
tricked the brain into thinking it was seeing

seamless movement as the viewer stared
through a tiny peephole and beheld the

gray-and-black image of a horse, galloping.
This is what I think about as I leaf through

the ads for flat-screen TVs in today's paper
or click a button on my phone to watch

a video posted from a pub in Ireland. Aren't
we lucky that we have no idea how primitive

our lives will seem one day? How appalling
to realize that our best cures for cancer will

look like a form of torture and that we really
thought we couldn't be everywhere at once.

Too Much Luck

Sometimes winning is effortless—you spin
the bottle, and it points to the right one.

You and he go off into the shadows
together and emerge with three children,

a lovely house, a dog, season tickets
to the Guthrie, and a little cabin

up north. Sometimes all of the cards are right—
you gather up the hand you're dealt, and you're

living in London, just off Kensington
High Street, and one day you're on the platform,

waiting for the Circle to Victoria,
when he sits down next to you, and glancing

at the play you're reading, quotes Rosalind—
some lines you had never noticed before.

Or perhaps you are shooting clay pigeons,
and it is the first time you've held a gun—

imagine that every time you yell "pull,"
you simply turn and make a perfect shot,

and you do this over and over, and
all the men grow very silent, watching,

until at last you miss a shot, which you
do on purpose, knowing how much luck costs.

The Signal

We were talking about how
things come easily to us
some days, not always—

sometimes we sit, staring out
the window and there's nothing—
just a blue sky without

a cloud of thought, an empty nest,
all the sweet birds lately gone.
You said there seems to be more

out there than ourselves,
something beyond our minds,
sending out a signal. Yes, I said,

I get that, and when that happens
we just go with the flow—remember
when we were all saying that?

Go with the flow—
that's how I ended up here,
sitting on a deck, looking out

on the hundred-acre marsh,
the last of the big willows down,
its hollow heart cracked,

all the branches splayed across
the lawn. Something
tells me I am more like

the willow than the sky,
something is saying hurry,
hurry—no, stop!

The Fortune Cookie Writer

On the cbc, he admitted
that he was behind on the job.

No one knew how hard he worked
to find just the right fortune

for each cookie, but mostly he
had been happy, letting his mind

drift among the clouds or
float like a leaf on the river

listening to the current,
translating what it said into

something that would make
a beautiful woman smile as

she slipped it into her pocket
and then into the glass bowl

on the windowsill where she
kept the fortunes that came to her

over the years, and which she
would sometimes read over—as if

they were love letters written
by someone she once knew.

Eleanor Beardsley in Paris

"There are no newspapers in Paris today"
she reports—"all part of an ongoing

dispute between labor groups and the French
government over President François

Hollande's plan to overhaul the country's
labor policies." She says this in a voice

that has gone from English to French,
from one set of vowels to another, as if

she is our French cousin intoning the words
in a flat, bemused way that could only

come from having spent ages waiting
in line at the boulangerie; she says these

things in the weary voice of someone
who has covered elections, riots, student

demonstrations, the Tour de France,
and terrorist attacks in Paris and Brussels.

She says these things, too, in the voice of
someone who loves how all the windows

in Paris open up in the summer so that
the sound of plates and silverware blends

with the sound of someone playing the piano
or laughing down the cobblestone street.

Miracles

Sometimes I think of those stories
where people get healed

on the spot: the blind man sees,
the woman stops shaking,

the lame man walks, and
the dead come forth from the grave.

Even the raving lunatic has his
demons cast into a herd of pigs!

How amazing it must have been
to take that first step, to look across

the land to the trees on the horizon
and see (clearly) the bird on the branch,

its feathers dangling down. How
satisfactory to sit perfectly still.

It must be a shock to be
healed so suddenly, to find the thing

you thought would end you
ended, as if playing at the game of Life,

all the pieces back in the box,
starting over, or (as it might be)

to wake from a bad dream and find
the morning sun spilling into your

bedroom and everyone you loved
downstairs, alive and young again.

Chickadees

The winter we got the new windows,
with their adjustable disappearing
shades, I spent hours watching

the chickadees catapult themselves
in and out of the bushes
on the other side of the glass.

As always, it was a cold winter,
but the chickadees knew how to
adapt. They remembered

where they had hidden every seed,
and like winter bees, they knew
how to dream of summer.

Later, I saw them, resurrected
and glorious in the branches
of the burning bush—resplendent

in their down-layered jackets,
each one impeccably capped—
little bellhops in the Sky-Blue Hotel.

At Los Alamos

Later, driving to Albuquerque,
we could see the triangle-shaped
white of the Wedding Dress
but not the mesa where they built
Little Boy and Fat Man.

It was Oppenheimer who
suggested that place; he'd been
there when he was a kid, and
he'd fallen in love with the
mesas and the cliffs of fall.

Up the houses sprang, like
mushrooms; people with babies
were in luck; they could have
a washing machine in a town
that was not on the map.

We had lunch—tacos and beer—
in the next town down and went on
to Bandelier. How pleasant it was
to walk in the woods with the
deer and then climb into the sun

on wooden ladders like the ones
the ancestral people used to reach
their gentle caves. How quietly
the centuries passed under
a cloudless sky.

What the Music Required

When I came home
the radio was on, and my kitchen
was in the middle of an opera.

I was hungry,
but it was clear that
I couldn't settle for a bowl of cereal—

no, what I needed
was something Italian—
homemade pasta, rolled out and filled with

minced chicken,
sautéed in butter and mixed with
fresh ricotta, grated parmigiano, and nutmeg.

I understood that
I must stand at the counter
shaping each circle of pasta into a little hat,

and that I must
slip them into a broth, brought
gently to almost boiling until they were

al dente. I knew,
from what the cookbook said,
that fifteen cappeletti in a bowl of broth

should be sufficient,
though I was warned that
it might be tempting to eat more,

and that there were stories
of people who had eaten a hundred
little hats and were filled to the brim—

the way the opera
was filling up every corner
of the kitchen with one big fat crescendo.

So Close

I was so close to drowning, so close
to slipping under the surface into
the weeds at the bottom of the lake

that I could almost see the sun overhead
like a streetlight at the top of the world,
and I was so close to crashing on the highway

that time when I had just passed Jordan
listening to a Henry James novel
as I reached down for my coffee cup and

hit a patch of ice and spun a complete
circle at 65 mph, wondering
how it would feel to crash—I was that close,

and I was so close that night in Tieton,
standing on the sidewalk looking up at
the light in the row of lonely windows,

thinking that the man up there needed me,
which of course was a mistake (almost
a disaster), and it took me many

years to undo the damage; I couldn't
even see how close I'd come to being
like one of those little donkeys in Cornwall—

the ones they put down into the mine pits
and never bring up again, because if
they did, they'd rather die than go back down.

The Light Left On

But then it's the light
That makes you remember

—YEHUDA AMICAI

I haven't forgotten you,
but I also haven't remembered you
as often as I should. It is difficult enough
to find time for the living.

Today Amicai's lines made me think
about how you must have felt
knowing you would die soon,
that you would be pulled backward

through that opening none of us
remembers into something else (or
nothing at all). I felt such pity
for your helplessness—after all,

why you? Of all the people in
that huge room of everyone we know,
why were you the one who had to leave
the party early? It wasn't fair, it wasn't

fair—at least, I know that's what you
thought, and you felt angry and cheated
and maybe slightly bemused at your
damned luck. Listen, I'd like to say,

you aren't missing much, but you
would know that isn't true.
I miss you (that much is true)—
but not as much as you deserve.

II. Work

The Long Centuries

Sometimes my mother can't sleep at night.
I know this because it's one of the things

she tells me on email—that and the names
of people who've died this week. For years now

they've been leaving—sisters, brothers, friends
from her grade school days, the boy she clobbered

with a baseball glove and made his nose bleed,
the cousin who used to tease her about

her red hair, and the girls she went dancing with
after high school in the year or two before

she married my father. She thinks
of them and wonders how it feels

to sleep all through the night
and the long centuries after.

What He Doesn't Tell Us

Where he sleeps at night, what he eats,
when he plans to come home—if ever.

He doesn't say why he is there or what
he's looking for—if anything. We know

only one of the languages he speaks and
the name of no one that he knows there.

He doesn't tell us what he thinks about
the volcano's smoke in the east or the

ocean in the west; it's a mystery—
as are his plans for the future, which we

may or may not be a part of—he never
commits to being anywhere longer

than today, and when he goes you never
know if you'll ever see him again.

Work

I've gone to it the way some people go
to a lover or the bottle. I've slipped

into the harness of it, felt the buckles
snap around me, let the reins lay lightly

on my back. It steadied me, calmed me, saved
me from the edge of the pit, from the ledge.

Best of all when my hands were deep in soil,
when my foot was on the shovel, when the

sweat was in my eyes. Better that than
idleness, better down upon my knees

to please the thing they call the world, and yet
even better then sometimes to work the

lines, to lift the sounds—so clear and easy
they almost seem effortless—into place.

Hoeing Potatoes with My Grandmother

In spring, we planted with the waning of
the moon, two weeks after the last frost.

The seed potatoes went into the long
trench, eye-side up, buried in hills spaced

evenly along the row like towns
in Nebraska. All summer we worked

the field that stretched (it seemed) forever,
our hoes chopping through the gray crust

to the black earth. My grandmother's hoe
was light and sharp; mine was heavy and dull.

That was the first I ever knew about
being of use—how each stroke makes its own

kind of sharpening. That was when I first
learned to love a well-honed thing.

Horseshoes with Maurice

On Sundays, my father and
Maurice played horseshoes.

I loved to see them in their
white shirts and black slacks,

each carrying a pair of clanking
iron in their calloused hands,

stepping the left foot forward
swinging the right arm back—

and I loved the way the shoe went
twisting and turning through the air

like an acrobat in the circus
we never got to see—and the way

I knew, simply from the sound,
that it was another perfect ringer.

More of Everything

The people who made me possible
came from places in middle Europe,
riding steamships through the middle of
the nineteenth century. They didn't
always get their right names, and if
they wrote home, I never heard.

The people who made me possible
worked hard clearing the land, tree
by stump by prairie grass, hauling
rock off the fields and gravel to the
roads. They seldom stopped to consider
if here was better than over there—

wherever that was. If they regretted
anything, they didn't say, and they
didn't tell stories about the old country;
my people didn't make a fuss
about being born or dying early—
they always died early—which

explains why they loved weddings
and christenings, birthdays and
the Fourth of July—any time they could
sit at a picnic table listening to
a polka band, going back many
times for more of everything.

My Brothers

Grew up speaking their own language—
a system of one-liners and stories
known only to them, a secret history of
monumental deeds, the mythology
of a private and particular realm.

They had their own way of crossing a river,
of cutting down a tree and stacking wood.
They worked like maniacs, locomotives
off track, bulldozers loose on a mountain,
taking it down one hill at a time.

My brothers had their own kind of music,
not exactly bebop, not really jazz, some
strange combination of Chicago and
old-timey blues with a hint of polka,
horns blaring, working to a double high C.

They were never going to be farmers—my
father made sure of that; why would he
want them working from dawn to dusk like
he did? Gambling on the clouds? But what
were they going to be? That was the question.

My Mother Breaks Her Ankle

I was there when she broke her wrist
in Paris one night as we were walking.
I had just pointed out the art deco design

on one of the doorways across the street,
so I have always felt responsible because
she was looking up instead of down

where the pavement gave way to tree roots.
I thought she'd disappeared, but right away
she was up, embarrassed that she'd fallen,

saying that her wrist hurt a little, but we should
just carry on to someplace for dinner,
but I could tell—from the way she held her arm

like a bird with a broken wing—that we had
better get back to the flat and pack for home
which we did, and she always had a bump

on her wrist and liked to tell her friends
how that happened in Paris, so when I hear
she's broken her ankle on the ice by the garage,

I think, Why not Rome, Mom, why not Istanbul?

Snowmen at the Farm

Late March. He began making the snow men—
four brothers who stood together in the cold,
gathered at the edge of what used to be.

Each had a twig nose and fresh charcoal eyes;
some had hats, and one had a scarf. He found
that making snowmen made him happier

than he had been for weeks. He liked making
something out of nothing—something that would
melt away when the winds came from the South.

South. South of the Border. Down Mexico
Way. That was the song that was in his head
all the while he worked, an old song, a song

he taught his snow men to sing in four-part
harmony (and in their perfect Spanish).

Open

(For Betty, 1951–1967)

It was her last summer.
I sat on a pantry stool
she'd pulled under the light
in the middle of the kitchen.

She took up the big needle,
held an ice-cube behind my ear,
and said, "Hold still!"
while she casually
punctured my earlobes—

first one, then the other.
That's all I remember,
except that something in her
kept me from crying out.

I reach up and take
   the soft skin between
   my thumb and fingers
to rub the place that
has never closed.

Because of the Sun

My father stood with the white machine shed
at his back. He hit the ball into the air,

high enough so that any of us on
the lawn or the soft sand at the middle

of the yard or the shade under the elms
would have time to come running in,

yelling, "I've got it! I've got it!" But then
something would happen because of the sun,

and the ball wouldn't be there anymore,
and then the corncrib and the milk house

and the hay barn would disappear, and my
father—oh God, my handsome father!—

would vanish, and the whole spinning world
would falter on its axis and fall apart.

Prodigal

When I came home from the demonstrations
(where there was no peace), when I returned

to the farm after living in the city
(where there was no love), my father welcomed me

like the prodigal I was. He came from his shop,
brushing sawdust from his jeans, opening

his arms to take me into the future—
with all its anguish hidden from us then.

The planets realigned; the land unrolled
into the fields and woods I knew as a child.

Though the land was never really ours,
it was the place that I knew best: gravel

and dirt, rock by rock, and the yellow clay
I shaped into something to take away.

III. Again

The Last Apples

For I have had too much
Of apple-picking
—ROBERT FROST

How many times did my mother
send people home with a bag of apples,

and still there were too many for us to
make into pies and applesauce, too many

to peel, slice, and pack into jars for winter?
Who would have thought such abundance

would ever end? Not I, walking home from
school, eating an apple I picked on my way,

not my grandmother at the picnic table,
slicing apples into the stoneware crock,

and not my mother, choosing only
the best apples from the basket. Then who

was it who'd had enough of apple-picking?
Whose sleep is not troubled now?

Autumn Again

It is autumn again—
season of mists and all that
Keatsian color; the tiny gnats
and the mosquitoes hover
on the breeze; the geese—
who arrived in pairs one
Sunday in May—now fly
high in the October sky.

It is autumn again. My father
sits in his chair on the porch,
listening to the almost inaudible
sound of field choppers chopping
a field of corn he did not plant.
Soon he will be ninety.

I tell him about the fields I see
between Chaska and St. Peter,
how the cornstalks have gone
from green to gold, how
the ears hang down, heavy.

It is autumn. The grapes are ripe
and purple-black on the vine.
I break off a cluster and walk back
to the house, eating them slowly,
staining my fingers and lips with
juice both sharp and sweet.

Carrying Water to the Field

And on those hot afternoons in July,
when my father was out on the tractor
cultivating rows of corn, my mother
would send us out with a Mason jar
filled with ice and water, a dish towel
wrapped around it for insulation.

Like a rocket launched to an orbiting
planet, we would cut across the fields
in a trajectory calculated to intercept—
or, perhaps, even—surprise him
in his absorption with the row and the
earth turning beneath the blade.

He would look up and see us, throttle
down, stop, and step from the tractor
with the grace of a cowboy dismounting
his horse, and receive gratefully the jar
of water, ice cubes now melted into tiny
shards, drinking it down in a single gulp,
while we watched, mission accomplished.

Stay

Don't die today, I said, looking
out at the marsh, at the tall reeds

and the blackbirds gathering in
the smallest box elder. Don't die,

I said, listening to music filling
the house, thinking of how we talked

on the phone last week and you told
me something I'd never heard before.

Stay for another year, another decade,
I said. Stay until the stars fall out

of the sky, until the oceans cover
the mountains—stay forever, or if

you have to go, don't let it be today,
while the corn is ripening in the fields.

What We Didn't Talk About

Everything. How we lived
on this planet under the trees

of our time without ever
saying how much we loved

the tallest apple at the
center of the orchard

back in the plentiful days
when the yellow pie-apples

filled basket after basket
and those small trees near

the grapevines—the ones
you don't remember planting—

were heavy with apples
that crunched at every bite,

and we didn't say anything
about how whenever we went

in or out of the yard we had
to pass the crooked pine tree,

giving it the secret words,
which were "back soon"

and it has been years since
we mentioned the elms

that your father (we didn't
talk about him either) set out

on the grassy side of the woods
to shelter the cows from rain

and heat, but we did talk about
the cows—at least we talked

about them—and how they
used to come through

the woods in the early morning
wearing a path in the loamy black

dirt that was our land, which is
another thing we didn't talk about.

My Father, Dying

It was hard work, dying, harder
than anything he'd ever done.

Whatever brutal, bruising, back-
breaking chore he'd forced himself

to endure—it was nothing
compared to this. And it took

so long. When would the job
be over? Who would call him

home for supper? And it was
hard for us (his children)—

all of our lives we'd heard
my mother telling us to go out,

help your father, but this
was work we could not do.

He was way out beyond us,
in a field we could not reach.

After You Were Gone

We found it hard to breathe—
as if a great stone

invisible to the world
had been placed on our hearts.

We moved through the world
as people do—we did all

the things that people do:
the phone rang, we answered it.

There was a knock at the door,
we opened it. Finally, we

stopped trying to explain.
All the words we had for things

were empty. It took a long time
to have something to say.

Sunday Afternoon in Early May

The afternoon is mostly green and
yellow—though otherwise unbloomed,

half-blossomed on the bare branch,
heavy with birdsong falling from

every part of the sky, carried up
by the corners like a cloth of blue

altogether threaded with sunlight and
wind. I talk across the miles to where

my mother reads slowly from a book
of ancient recipes: one for mending bones,

one for headache, and one for love that
was lost for reasons no one remembers.

Mother, mother, tell me what I should do,
with the wind, the birds, and the sky so blue.

Reading Anna Swir in October

My suffering / is useful to me.

Now I understand why my friends
kept mentioning her name, and yes

I would like something useful
to come out of this.

I open my hand and there's
a bruise; I don't know where it

came from. I open my heart
and there's a riddle; I don't know

the answer. I can't remember
how it felt to be young,

and then I do. After that I
can tell you anything.

For the Letter Writers

For those who have lived by
the stroke of the pen, by ink

gathered in the curve of a letter,
for those whose words have filled pages,

for the plain hands of the mothers,
reporting the quotidian news of

the day (as in how many quarts
of applesauce, how many baskets

of wash on the line), and for the
dignified script of the fathers,

carrying the terrible news,
but most of all for the lovers

whose letters went into the fire,
(and never spoke a word).

Without

Often, I want to return to my old body.

—HIEU MINH NGUYEN

Tell me about it. How you returned
to what you already had,

to what you (even now,
at this moment, alive) have,

and I will tell you how I returned
each morning to mine, remembering friends

who were once heartbreakingly beautiful
and now are gone, gone from the riverbanks,

the moonlit cafés, and gone from the rooms
where they once bent over a page

writing words like these.
Tell me, if you can,

how it is to be without,
to be lighter than air.

How I'm Doing

Sometimes the shaking stops,
my handwriting loosens, and I have
a moment of pure stillness.

I don't forget the other thing.
I don't pretend I'll be spared the
usual humiliations.

For many years, age was just a coat
I wore, though lately I see how tattered
it's become—a paltry thing.

I have many friends on that other
shore—singing, counting swans,
gathered at the river to wave to us

as we pass by in our cars, the radio filled
with voices disappearing
into the rearview mirror.

Isla, Morning

Bird of no name perched
on the top of the palm tree,
at the tip of the palapa,

you are my island alarm clock!
You are my father's voice
calling me to help with the chores

even though the barn is empty,
even though the milkers no longer
hang in the milk house,

even though we're both
in lands we never knew.

Your Name

One day, when you were no longer
there, I forgot to say your name.
I say it now. Your name

is more beautiful than the sky
at dawn—the bowl of it fills up
with colors only air can hold.

I hear your name on the prairie,
coming from beyond the farthest
field, the last line of trees—your name

is the only thing that can prove
that the ear can hear beyond the grave.
I say your name, and you answer

with a silence that I take
for love—a love that I carry
all the way to the horizon.

Making Do

The days were long. Money floated away
on the river or the wind carried it.

We were being relieved of a great weight,
but at the time we did not understand.

We had become so accustomed to what
we did not need that for a while we thought

it was what we wanted, but we were wrong.
What we really wanted, it turned out, was

a song—just a good old song to get us
through, something that we could sing together

sitting out on the porch (suddenly there
were porches again) while the children played

Red Rover in the long grass of the lawns
in front of houses, their doors opened wide.